OINTMENT WEATHER
AF445226
OINTMENT WEATHER
MARCH 2024 — APRIL 2025

OINTMENT

INSURGENT POIETICS
FOR DESPERATE TIMES

WEATHER

THOM EICHELBERGER-YOUNG

QUEEN. Good Hamlet cast thy nightly colour off,

And let thine eye looke like a Friend on Denmarke.

Do not for euer with thy veyled lids

Seeke for thy Noble Father in the dust;

Thou know'st 'tis common, all that liues must dye,

Passing through Nature, to Eternity.

HAM. I Madam, it is common.

QUEEN. If it be;

Why seemes it so particular with thee.

HAM. Seemes Madam? Nay, it is: I know not Seemes:

'Tis not alone my Inky Cloake (good Mother)

Nor Customary suites of solemne Blacke,

Nor windy suspiration of forc'd breath,

No, nor the fruitfull Riuer in the Eye,

Nor the deiected hauiour of the Visage,

Together with all Formes, Moods, shewes of Griefe,

That can denote me truly. These indeed Seeme,

For they are actions that a man might play:

But I haue that Within, which passeth show;

These, but the Trappings, and the Suites of woe.

[Ham. 1.2.255-67]

contents

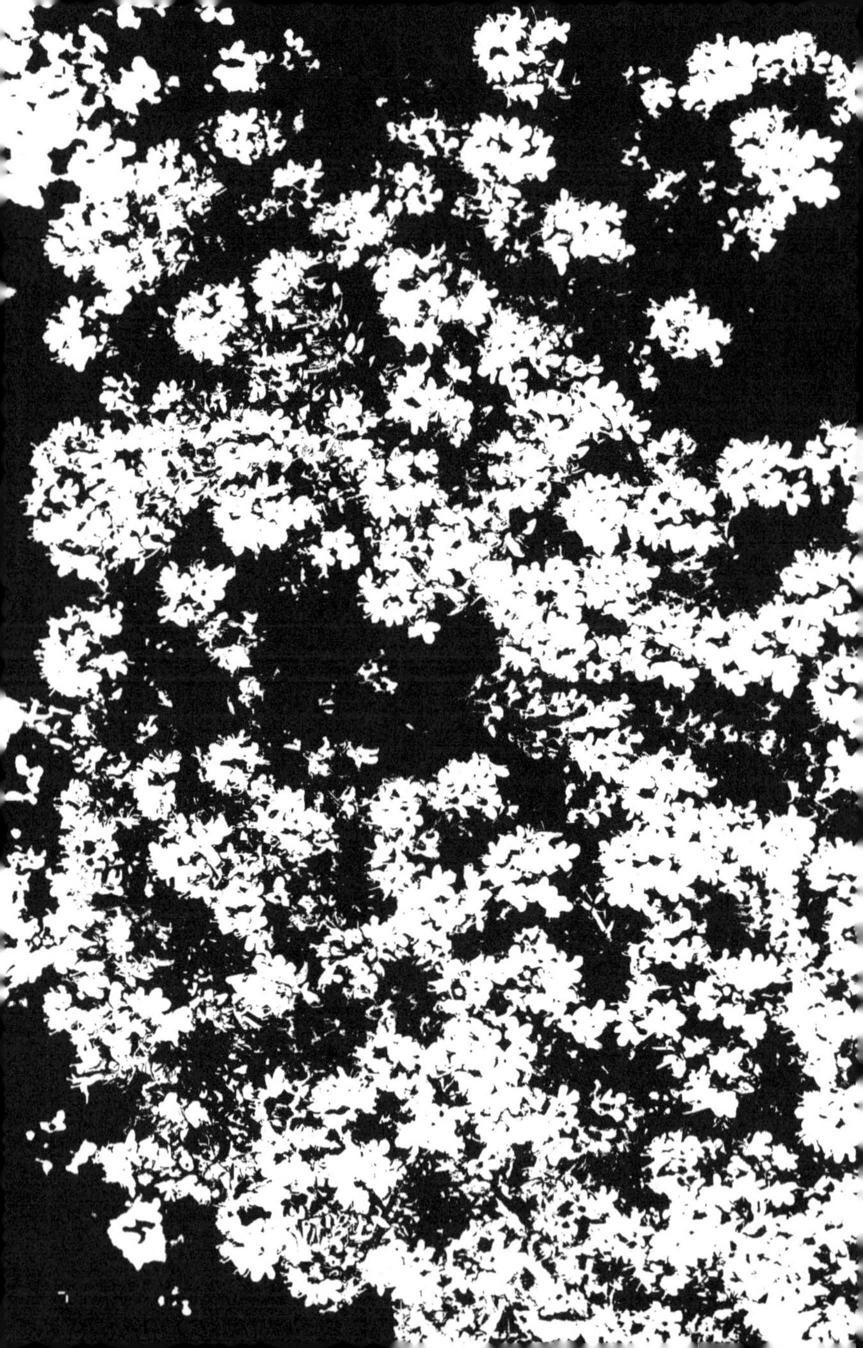

TRADE WINDS | PORN SEQUENCE

WHEN I WRITE FICTION, IT IS TYPICALLY TWO STEPS away from my being / If I am in the kitchen, the story will occur in the garden—I am no longer preparing food, but cultivating the herbs I will cook with later / I also do not have a garden / I have, however, maintained the conversation or thought in my head within the story taking place not in the kitchen, where it came to me, but instead in the garden / Life-writing can be this way: when you change a name, you take a step away from **reality** [realitas] / I know a writer who publishes memoirs about raising foster children under a pseudonym, but they show up in person at readings—which leaves me wondering about the slim statistical margin where the people whose domain creates the need for the pseudonym attend the reading in question and the pseudonym is unmasked in the worst, most violent, way / Her husband walks into a seminar (this is real, they both teach at a university, in a department with a problematic tendency to hire couples—of which there are some five or six) one morning and announces her pseudonym to the class—another strike / But, this is also an instance in my own life of a **well-kept secret** that has become an **open secret** / and I will not mention any other friends who made this information transparent to me well before her husband walked into the seminar

⌒

Operating against the grain—**alt-def: anthimeria [anti-meros]** / The etymological process by which the word **secret** became a noun is no "chicken or egg" conundrum—the verb came first / from the Latin **se+cernere=to set apart** / The secret is knowledge set aside from various aspects of publicized discourse / Some secrets are family secrets / Secret languages held between twins or childhood friends / Some are sexy secrets between lovers / Some secrets we [try to] hide from ourselves / Some are violent war crimes the government attempts to secret away, encrypted in [▓▓▓▓▓▓]

⌒

How does this work? / Close listening! / *The EXTENDING tool is an implant designed for Samsung F Series Smart Televisions. The implant is designed to record audio from the built-in microphone and egress or store the data* [1] / The television is implanted with the device through a USB [2] / a popular tool for streaming television or entertainment on a television (television as metonym of cable is an ever weaker **system of definition**) is the Amazon FireStick, which operates via USB mounted to the smart television. Other devices include Optisigns Android Stick Player, Samsung FitPlus, Watch ONN, etc. / Osama Bin Laden circumvented such technology designed to surveil individuals like him, whom—like it or not—cannot avoid the corporatist-imperial state's technological exports when producing their revolutionary actions, no matter where located [departure from this an affordance to another, vital, conversation]. His house at Abbottabad was *not* connected to the internet. When I read Osama Bin Laden's letters on the Director of National Intelligence website [3], I am amazed to learn the rhetorical strategies and operations at play bear intense similitude to 'our' own—so familiar, too, of the Appalachian Kirby-Eller family whose letters and diaries I helped produce the metadata for when working in a regional archive. Bin Laden's letters are plaintive, at times invoking, poetically, a god who ordains this miraculous natural world—speaking into the intensity of the subaltern difference with the cultural "center" manifested via Imperialism / In a letter to his sister [4], Bin Laden begins

> *In the name of God the merciful the passionate. Thanks to God the Lord of the heavens and prayers and greetings on our Prophet Muhammad and on kindred and all his followers. Thereafter: To my beloved sister Um 'Abd-al-Rahman, may God save. I send my message. I write this message to you, asking God that you and those who are with you are in good status and healthy in your religion and in your daily life. I convey to you the good news of meeting with you, which was long awaited, thank God. I also convey the good news of a dream seen by Khalid, after my message to you on[…] God knows that we did not write until after the extreme feeling of embarrassment from you and for our delay*

/ The issue is the cultural production of the enemy in the (our) Imperialist state—in November of 2023, CNN ran an article with the headline *Some Young Americans on TikTok Sympathize with Osama Bin Laden.* An excerpt:

> *In one video no longer available on the platform that had been viewed more than 1.6 million times, a New York-based*

lifestyle influencer encouraged others to read the letter and said, "if you have read it, let me know if you are also going through an existential crisis in this very moment, because in the last 20 minutes, my entire viewpoint on the entire life I have believed, and I have lived, has changed.

The CNN article is a disturbing index point in the fascistic and nationalistic tendencies promulgated in the corporate media landscape that captures Americans' attentions. An early paragraph implicitly criticizes while describing how the letter "Justifies the targeting and killing of Americans," a self-reflexive bias that is in tandem with minimized reporting and biased coverage regarding US-funded genocidal and warmongering the world over, heavily active at CNN. The United States spends substantial resources making these exact same justifications, as well as machines of war and pioneering digital frontiers towards the efficient targeting of 'enemy combatants.'

The situational paradigm which concerns the 'American Citizen' in these conflicts, and which bears media attention, surrounds the pool of victims—some near 3,000 in 9/11, equated with the 1,195 killed on October 7th. As punishment for these egregious losses, tens and hundreds of thousands of civilians are eliminated—as we see in Gaza.

Americans are generally incapable of recognizing the double-edged sword that is their government (generally but) rhetorically. Even where anti-American energies and commentaries are promoted, as with Bin Laden's, addressed at anti-people actions by the government of the United States, such is elided—I am thinking of where Bin Laden or others have carefully qualified their statements as being towards the imperialist oppressor who is actively oppressing *us*. It is a choice to associate with the enemy-state, thus—America—ignoring the entirety of the conversation or political/historical dynamics.

(Because I write and document) I have little sympathy to mainstream media organizations as they suffer threats from the incoming Trump administration—already weaponizing the legal system to cast the censorious threat of crippling lawsuits which could collapse a newsroom for a small publication if they critique Trump—and bemoan the possibility of State sponsored censorship. These same organizations—the Media—have already been the functional arm of censorship and propaganda, manipulating civilians with minimal time to afford for self-educating within a paradigmatically information-overload driven system of life. They bear essential responsibility for failing to inform, while manipulating a technology—journalism—that is perceived as trustable. You quite rarely hear the reportage of journalists active in Gaza and other hotbeds of crisis—unless you find alternative media venues not operated by typically conventional media organizations. Look at the Writers Against the War on Gaza *New York War Crimes* production against readership and use of *The New York Times*, as but one instance of this dynamic, reflecting the inviability of contemporary mass media, coming about in response to industrial-corporate failures that persist in their dissemination and sprawl. / So: if not outright state media, the corporate controlled "journalism" remains a nationalist media [5]—meanwhile, the readers of Bin Laden's "Letter to America" are reacting to similarly manifesting rhetorical strategies and effective styles [designs to persuade] of State media programming and diction in Bin Laden's communications / The Imperialists, via their media arms, have always portrayed only the worst facets of their enemy, distorting them from their actions-into-events for a turn instead into propagandistic fantasies which realize their agendas.

And, who is an Imperialist but those who seek to maintain the status quo of the government of the United States? Thus, left and right regardless—those speaking into the support for a political party and agenda—these are Imperialists. Voters in the United States seeking to maintain sensations of democratic comfort within their terrain while other people are blasted into non-existence with the funding of tax payer dollars. These are Imperialists. The primary vehicle for this discourse is the mainstream media. The left-wing & party-aligned [Democratic] frustration with Donald Trump [6] emerges in part from liberals' intense history of platforming him prior to his far-right rhetorical shift, a shift which was paired with intense continuous publicization and re-production by such as CNN, NBC, and ABC, of Trump's rhetoric on a daily basis, near hourly, probably to the minute, as well as afterwards—their consistent misprision being attacks upon what he *says he will do* while covering their faces to the actions of the Obama and Biden administrations— as has happened nigh on consistently with party advocates during the current administration.

Imperialist [Nationalist thus] Americans have ignored hearing any holistic sense [of what is happening]. Such sense would say the enemy is no longer the object enemy [in-amicus] but is actually a speaking subject [sub-jacere] [7] and such too that recently I am certain I read somewhere Juliana Spahr (I think) expresses frustration at the news for not explicating the reasons behind suicide bombings [8]—certainly individuals do not blow themselves up in a vacuum.

So, what is it we were *not* told that explains this? We want to know why, and the *not* which faces us is capacious—manifesting itself as monumental, possibly even universal. Americans—adhered to the system of their governance—seek to deny this universal—the first fact of their nation's waged destruction.

The *not* is the child of programming an enculturating system of capital and the viral impacts of such-in-commodification upon subalternated societies [in name of spreading 'democracy'], taking place within the contradictorily violent contemporaneous horizon of war-peace we are forced to exist in [9] (rampantly accelerating through the World Wars as we hurtled towards the temporal realization of the 'forever war' and the specter of the 'final war'/World War III) /

∩

Within the technology found in his compound, the US soldiers who will kill Osama Bin Laden find a *stash of pornography* which has been heavily disparaged and memed (that the media wouldn't ever be able to handle holistic [alt-def: syncretic or interdisciplinary] representation regardless) / Then, there is this email located at Wikileaks by Scott Stewart, an intelligence analyst at Stratfor and former government operative—*intelligence analysis* reads *lies* and *superficiality* and *what I will not say* and asks the question *Why won't you say this?* / A "bro" submits a FOIA request essentially demanding a catalog record (alt-def: finding aid) of Bin Laden's porn collection

I personally believe us dudes have a right to know what the world's most wanted man masturbated to. I think something like that should enter the public record. Like... what if it turned out he exclusively watched white, male, American porn stars? Wouldn't that be anathema to his beliefs? Wouldn't that be an interesting thing to learn about the man? [10]

The Washington Post quotes this statement: *he believes "us dudes" have a "right to know what the world's most wanted" was watching. "Like… what if"* [11]

Re: [CT] Indonesian terror suspect had porn stash

Email-ID	1905781
Date	2011-05-19 15:49:37
From	scott.stewart@stratfor.com
To	ct@stratfor.com, sean.noonan@stratfor.com

Re: [CT] Indonesian terror suspect had porn stash

I can't say this in the stuff I write, but I personally believe that sexual repression is a huge factor in the recruitment and formation of jihadists - especially the young suicide bombers.

They get way too fixated on the idea of the 72 perpetual virgins. It is only one element of the Muslim vision of paradise, but it is the one they most focus on.

Another Stratfor email (an "all-call" to staff) presents the pornography issue in a radically different line—reading between the lines either a link(age) between Obama and Osama (the Islamophobic desired off-homonymity of the Right [here grasping at a murky shibboleth near-articulated]) or an incoherent mess(age) of moral decay and co-opted ideologies for self-aggrandizement and capital accrual; save that the anger of the communicating party here is not at the unfair locus of capital in wealthy classes (the elite) but that the parties in question (sender and recipients) are "outsiders" within the current State apparatus and are dissatisfied in their capital accrual thus far—seeking to deploy a scapegoat to eradicate their blame.

[Custom Intelligence Services] United States of Pornography

Released on 2012-10-17 17:00 GMT

Email-ID	490272
Date	2011-06-23 02:59:45
From	machsid77@gmail.com
To	service@stratfor.com

[Custom Intelligence Services] United States of Pornography

Mach sent a message using the contact form at
https://www.stratfor.com/contact.

Hello,

Big Email. Please read all statements.

An American said to me that 200 million Americans are involved in pornography. Is this true?

World Pornography is $158 Billion every year. If you view porn you are involved in pornography.

Majority of internet servers and Google servers are located in USA but there is no serious actions from USA to shut down world porn.

10,000 Rapes in 5 days. Obama is Responsible for this.

George Friedman, Stratfor CEO, offers this assessment of his employee's freedom of communication and speech:

> *God knows what a hundred employees writing endless emails might say that is embarrassing, stupid or subject to misinterpretation. … As they search our emails for signs of a vast conspiracy, they will be disappointed* [12]

though Scott Stewart was still employed at Stratfor until 2020 before leaving to work for TorchStone Global / Another email at Stratfor notes the working relationship between Stratfor and TorchStone Global is very positive [productive (to a capital telos)], with many transplants leaving Stratfor for the "good money" at TorchStone Global—intelligence vs. money or is there a hero complex saying *I deserve the world for saving it supposedly?*

Re: TorchStone featured in Forbes Magazine

Released on 2013-11-15 00:00 GMT

Email-ID	2953720
Date	2011-11-06 22:22:42
From	burton@stratfor.com
To	burton@stratfor.com, kuykendall@stratfor.com, oconnor@stratfor.com, shea.morenz@stratfor.com

Re: TorchStone featured in Forbes Magazine

Only Protective Intelligence monitoring. You can make a lot of money, but
its not publishing. I've given Frank at TorchStone a good number of jobs
and he wants me for his board, but I really don't have the time.
Sent via BlackBerry by AT&T

From: Shea Morenz <shea.morenz@stratfor.com>
Date: Sun, 6 Nov 2011 15:17:23 -0600 (CST)
To: Fred Burton<burton@stratfor.com>; Don
Kuykendall<kuykendall@stratfor.com>; Darryl O'Connor<oconnor@stratfor.com>
Subject: Re: TorchStone featured in Forbes Magazine
Interesting business... btw, do we do any security consulting? Guessing it
would be a separate biz from CIS and more tailored from Tactical team?
--
Shea Morenz
Managing Partner
STRATFOR

Keyword search: "Pornography"

Deployed operation site: Wikileaks

Yieldings: 7,393 results

Desired/Expected report format: data analysis.

Operative: a citizen

I am in an archive discovering dark histories that I was only vaguely aware of having been documented. Obliqued. I read emails where links are merely forwarded not with an empathy or a sympathy, but something else I feel as malicious connection—say in the *schadenfreude* moments when relishing in the pain of the other [that we can recognize the impetus and emotion of these structures not only as behavioral pattern but as reflexive mechanisms of our own (at times) deployments] / One Stratfor email forwards a link from a Chinese newspaper (*Shanghai Daily*) reporting the detention of 32 women for operating a gay pornographic fiction website / (I am in an archive) / A further cursory google search of the phrase "China Detains 32 women for gay porn website" yields the following results

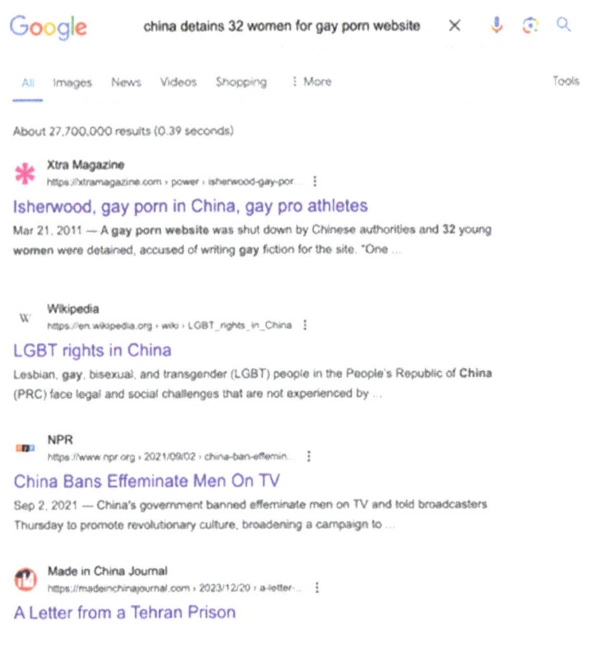

Only one document emerges from the search for **EXACT PHRASE** "gay pornography" and it is the above-mentioned Stratfor thread. In a reply in the thread, Sean Noonan, a tactical analyst at the firm, writes of the detained women that what they'd have earned *would be a pretty good wage if they actually got paid*

Searching "gay porn" reveals 64 results, many of which are duplicated as the terms repeat in threads or documents—and in this instance, the "HBGary" emails all return an INTERNAL SERVICE ERROR when clicked through. Instead, this viewer stumbles across a listserv or forum aggregating a survey of child porn censorship by covert forces within the Italian State, documenting how the censorship mechanisms fold in various authenticated, viable, and legal adult homosexual community websites especially related to activism, pornography [of adults], or both / Another email thread discusses a linked article to the Gadhafi family DVD collections, including a gay porn title / Another Stratfor thread is full of sexual jokes between coworkers and makes light of a gay coworker possibly watching gay pornography while working from home / Another Stratfor thread discusses an intelligence source and their rundown of Russian spies weaponizing various types of pornography against foreign embassy workers within Russia—including *gay if you are straight*

∩

The majority of the 1,730 search results for the keyword "transgender" are in the DNC email dump, or otherwise results from shared articles produced and related to issues in the United States. Other examples, related to various legislative acts around the world repressing gender identity and freedom of gender expression and identification, are included on rare occasion [though few denote the landscape of the United States of America: an escalating hostile terrain to transgender individuals]

⌒

FUTURE PRAXIS: Wikileaks/Leaked textual concordances—assessing and preparing orders of magnitude for moral and legislative issues of concern through expositions of various governments' and State forces' communications practices as a means to demonstrate these States' bearing of the mantle of moral and ethical devastation [13] as well as the adherence to this State alignment by a far wider consideration of an 'uncritical' Imperialist American speaking subject [here under indictment] and their relationship to various mainstream and covert media.

ALONG THE SIDE OF MY MANUSCRIPT / THIS IS NOT
marginality / Over story or layer / Remembering that the screen is not my own space / not matter—what we put on it [14] / I hope to universalize this, but instinctually collapse to the self again / It is, afterall, within my sight, that it is **on sight** / which some may mistake for a British-English construction / It is not / Anyway / **Try out experimental AI features Get help writing, organizing tabs and creating custom themes [No Thanks] [Continue]** / I suspect **[No Thanks]** is not the end of the story /

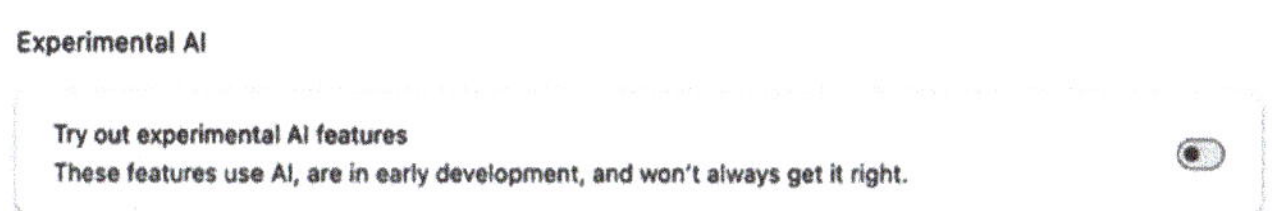

That's my screen when I select **[Continue]** / This sequence becomes a weather urging me indoors—to go find a poem by Rae Armantrout / To find the poem, I will take the following actions: get off the sofa [purchased at an employee sale when I was working ███████████ ████—dreadful days (of everyone's [that are in this way] stories)], walk across the "living room" [whose history is explored thoroughly in volumes such as Bill Bryson's *At Home*], walk up the stairs [which will connect to my reactive airway disease—being a chronic smoker], and look at the second shelf up on the left most bookshelf against the wall in the office [there are [WERE] four bookshelves, and books are [WERE] piled on top of them several feet high to the ceiling, as well as starting to take up layers on each shelf (Eyes / memorize to memorialize [trajectory of the event of sight] / —I do not live there anymore, now her books sit here next to Clark Coolidge's on the second shelf up of the third book case from the right wall of my office)—Rae's books do [DID] this to my own books—covering the books behind; stacks of books, as can be expected, appear throughout various heavily trafficked areas of the house: I typically stand and admire STOOD AND ADMIRED in THAT room (now I like to look at the Buffalo streets), where I WAS actually a collector, when I leave the room, the material transitions—by occupational status now, I am a reader, and then in incorporating it I am a poet and a thinker, and by professional affiliation I am a poet-scholar.

The poet and the thinker, *making*—in this po[i]ethics—are interchangeable and oriented at universalizing access to the experience of being. This is the urgent matter of all time and energy, especially as it relates to the sufferings and necessities [15] [for living] of bodies who are mandatorily prohibited by law and order from speaking and access to full participation in society.

The poet-scholar role, however, positions me within a technological discourse [16] upon a single track that is totally organized around exegetical theses of a self-assertive nature, reflexively anticipating the need to defend and own an interpretation [driven by the commodification of discourse through the university system]. And, still, there is the hybridity occurring within the movement across all three outputs. These points *matter*—as points of disclosure, considering I am a student in the Poetics Program at SUNY Buffalo, engaging in the university dynamic despite my critique of the university's institutional status—what you *can* [reading/receiving] expect in regards to the syntactical framing of this book is thus inevitable /

Before I take/took these actions, this half-remembered poem by Armantrout reminds me (anticipating an analysis later) of the weeks when I interviewed my grandmother (who was my best friend) and was curious to poke and prod about her 93 year life, during which the microwave, television, space shuttle, and suicide drone swarm were invented—she was generally unimpressed [read: unafraid], though provided visceral narrative memories of her own experiences as an athlete, which itself becomes more important when remembering it as clarification that my grandmother wanted to stress her participation in the liberation of women, despite her otherwise conservatism, and she was quite proud of her college education and athletic recognitions / I am revising this and struck with the awareness of the way Helen Thomas [my grandmother in question] was conducting/revising/ascribing her own history / [Unreliable narration—you must believe me]

Armantrout's poem is called "Screen Memory" and is in the 2020 collection *Conjure* / I can immediately identify it in the Table of Contents / I could also quote the poem in full / But, I wrote this before other realizations / What I remember, however, seems important / *My screen claims I have "new memories"* [17] / and I wonder / what if the line read *My screen claims:* "I have new memories" / Do you see the connection? [18]

∩

This is the imagined nightmare / What words do not foresee / There is nothing to foresee [—despite the intentions of software such as COMPAS to provide ("rehabilitated" prisoner) recidivism scores in an alignment or march towards a *Minority Report* society here untethered to psychic revelations delivered to mediums but instead upon a neutralized, universal approach of 'what-could-be-will-be' witnessed in the total-applications of another media program such as *Logan's Run*] / When one does not anticipate what is / what is a lie [lugiz] / I do not know if both have ideas

∩

Right now occurs a disastrous debate wherein [███████ █████] has publicly lied [their modus operandi], and I am learning alongside anyone on the radio [listening in]—

claiming she lives on the other side of the country [which was just destroyed] / claiming [████████████████] / I walk around the room / incapable in the situation of reducing it to one of "the" and not their pronoun / It is extremely— / Does the other person deserve the position on this board / It is extremely upsetting—I am extremely upset / There are feelings that begin in the middle of you / [████████████████████] / Request [████████████████] / Thumbs move up / The middle of the body is the symbolic location of the stomach / See also: **solar plexus** the **celiac plexus** the radiant knowledge that began in the center of *you* / "Thank god"—I am now quoting from Susan Howe's diaries, where I learn she is religious in 1993 / Thank god for the smooth voice of the radio DJ behind the[se] scenes / *The board of directors is made up of nine individuals but must act as one in unison* / Has anyone read William Gaddis' *J R* recently? / I still enjoy it all these years / The school in the novel has an internal CCTV system which also operates an aspect of surveillance— early surveillance entailed the assurance that a single voice was present, and capable of articulating authority / Earlier surveillance technologies involved watchers looking away from their communities and *for* or *towards* [potential] others on their horizon against whom they'd light beacons that transmitted their surveilled sight backwards as warnings / Now, with developed camera technology, the direction of the observed has shifted inside the community to ensure that every passerby can be indexed and known to an algorithm / Q: How do you interact with others? / &the things come up rapidly / *Nine people who have to come together and make a decision can be quite challenging* / She says and every answer is a cookie-cutter / She suggests in being kind above all, but she has texted during the debate critical statements of the opponent's home and on-camera background, and elsewhere documented her annoyance at attention to genocides across the planet because of her incapacity to recognize a matrix of post-[natural] disaster local interactions with the abroad crises or mimetic experiences within her locality which would otherwise extrapolate the urgency of the situations alterior to her own—the selfish neoliberal gene [& radiance of her Imperialism] / Disparaging / There is churning within the belly [belig from OG/koiliakos becoming celiac/ they are both abdominal] / The only way I have ever put this / *I do love vigorous discussions—and I do love when we all laugh later* / and but so *really it is important to include diverse opinions and that is a deficit of this board* / Thank you— / *Can you answer that* / and *I did already* /

∩

The situation is a mess—is this message something to bring me out of this sequence? / A different tack we have not taken so far / service to community / in terms of / it is important to / not to be complacent / in terms of contributing / to the community / we can always improve / and have community engagement / and more opportunities / and *especially since the pandemic* [people love to say that] (their **since** being an uneven uncertainty between **after** and **within**) / and that's the main / and I say that / repeat the / and it was / how do you feel about / current level / well institutional memory / twenty years ago / has not improved / I always felt / since we had the reach / we used to have offices / ▮▮▮▮▮▮▮▮ / ▮▮▮▮▮▮ / Volunteer organizations / frequencies and more interactions / business communities / ▮▮▮▮ ▮▮▮▮▮ / has not grown presence / as much as I had hoped and having / eight years ago / folding it all into one / I think that was a *civil* / *a symbol* / and I would like to reverse that / Fantastic / We see Dennis / Does that mean / We have a call / on the line / and the voice of the smooth DJ comes back in—the caller breathes heavily, *I am calling as a previous board member* / to wit is a prolonged discussion and then questions about the inability of the community in question to actually foster—now suddenly, the scene shifts and I believe the disaster may run a different direction / Suddenly the opponent informs that they were banned eight years ago, and discusses how coming back *includes a lot of forgiveness and alignment with the mission statement because I do believe in [███████████'s] values* / And also *I do thank you for your work in the past on the board* / Some one else mentions complete dedication / and I know that a situation occurred wherein a racial slur was used by someone in this communtiy at a radio event / *Both of your minds and hearts are very devoted* / [TO THE CAUSE] / *there are two wonderful people* / this is a **LIE** / framed differently / but spoken the exact same as the other big lie / The smooth DJ returns to the situation / another caller arises / Many people are disgruntled by the introduction of the revolutionary—what this situation is overall about, to expand upon it from the personal into the theoretical—

angered that "not enough" / *You have an agenda—certain things you want to get done* / But the work right now is not about this—this is about the expansion of consideration currently and labors that were [then] performed—the polis is approving of this in reaction to the revolutionary sentiment / That is the drawback of grand ideas, ultimately, in terms of an audience / There is something Ted [Pearson] has said about strikes against people—one of his is the polis voting for Trump [now three times] / that's something that trickles down / *Excuse us caller—Excuse me caller* / and *I was wondering if there was an accusation or a question* / and now *How at the end of the day are you going to come to that peaceful resolution where you can all come together and have a beer?* / You do not want to hear the intense answer—though it includes early on the line *Don't forget about the music* / The poem had ended when the question comes up *if both candidates are deemed dissatisfactory, will the election be drawn up again with new candidates* / It seems that shared context is felt across the airwaves

∩

There is a popular beach at the site of Marconi Station's wireless transmitter over the Atlantic Ocean where people enjoy various aquatic recreational activities / There is an urban legend that Guglielmo Marconi developed this magical or esoteric system of thinking wherein "no sound ever dies"—that sound waves reverberate forever and thus it is only a matter of time before equipment is developed to register these sounds and play them back (historiographical acoustics) / that we will hear the Christ was core to the thought or the dream / I wonder that this is not some form of embedded Christian narrative after all is said and done—vying to prove faith beyond the material application such fantastical equipment would afford (consider the viable usage it could entail in exonerating people) / In his dream, we will not hear the sounds of slaves, of wars the world over, of burning cities after conquest, we will not investigate crimes or dire mysteries. Marconi's dream is a legend of sheer and narcissistic fantasy—towards one-track thoughts upon the matter of utterances and their preservation, in demonstration of the problematics pervading the analytical lines of thought in works by J.L. Austin, Judith Butler, Lacan, [rattle off the list in the revisions or discussions], speech and language wherein lie excisions and ignorances [19] [often born of failures towards understanding (a) holistic representation] which deny the sovereignty and experiences of countless subjects outside a dominant experience codified into ideology hence—why no sane engineer has pursued technological expedition to this degree / However, as we have noted [20], substantial developments have been focused upon autonomous devices such as "Vision" from Ghost Robotics, which does incorporate radio technology—upon the cutting edge / Coincidentally to all that, I think of the **knife drone** / which is **my definition** / I recall waking up to news that al-Zawahiri was killed while watching *something* [being the sunrise (over Kabul)—like I am now (THEN) as I am revising—as part of his morning routine/practice/ meditation] on his balcony—his routine had been tracked and pinned down to such a degree as to be capable of firing an R9X missile at him / Nick Waters picks up the tale: *The R9X* [...] *destroys its target using its kinetic energy and six blades that are deployed from the missile before impact.* [21]

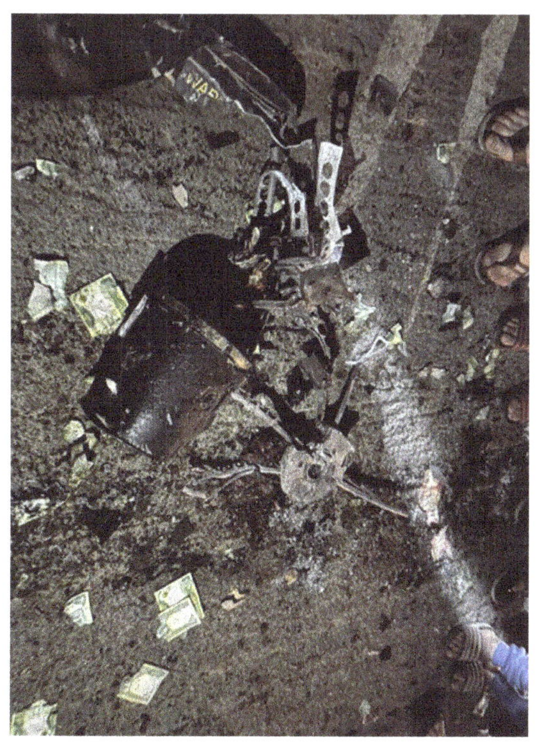

Ali Hashem's image showing remnants of an AGM–114r9x Hellfire missile. The blade system unique to this armament can be seen near the center. This photo was taken after a strike in Iraq, which killed Kata'ib Hezbollah drone unit commander Wissam AlSaedi, occurring on February 7th, 2024. Via OSMP.

Nearly a million fall run Chinook Salmon released into the Klamath River days ago and all have died after passing through existing infrastructure in iron gate dams, having incurred gas-bubble disease, which is a non-infectious environmentally induced trauma

The flow plus the drop creates gas bubbles inside the fish / they perish / *It was unexpected and unfortunate* / The State insists water quality was not at issue in the massive fish-kill / It was merely unfortunate that they passed through the lingering dam structure which had not been removed / With all the attention towards environmental study, why was there minimal awareness of extant infrastructure ahead of the first run? / Reports all guarantee that the infrastructure will be removed and that this was the first release / A calculus of experimentation / *for we actually had an abundance of fish, actually we had an additional 800,000* / is 830,000 dead salmon fry spoken of clinically and with hope for improvements to the system and engineered developments / *good news stories out of a really bad news story—but we will meet our fish goals this year* / One wonders that there is not frequent attention to the refrain: there will *not* be a shortfall in salmon supply in the food chain— [22]

26 students are killed at Tripoli's Military College in March of 2020 by a drone attack / *The site was attacked by a drone* [23] / The drone in question fired a missile which is manufactured in China / Such is indicated in fragments left behind / The report says this / The report is not the sound of the explosion, but the legacy of it / The report is not included in Marconi's dreams / The culpable party for the attack is stated to be Khalifa Haftar / Haftar's forces are directly supported by Russia / China funnels much money across African nations—or did, some State efforts have stalled—via their Belt and Road Initiative [24]/ In the warzone of Libya continuing today, Russia's influence has more dominance in potential / All the roads are gone / There was the store / Susan Howe dreams in her diaries of a blanket of her son's on Quartz Road in Guilford, CT— her son having been bitten earlier in this dream by a strange sea creature and then dying (though they expected him to survive) / and in the dream she is her son's "mommy" and sister / So, there was a blanket on the road / So, the cat curls up next to you / *I must go on*

Stanzas in divagation / Meditation on the thermocline / or das nichts / and questioning *what is coming from there* / The music shifts to a situation about dissipation / The obvious connection is about fish / **appropriate def: aquatic life** / v1: The Introductory System / A thermocline is a space between hot and cold water / CNN has 58 live updates to review the next morning after the State of the Union / 146 posts total / Live discussion is a fence under construction, from the real time event commencing to its finish / Such a fence is designed to limit interpretation / I can take pistachio halva with my coffee, but it will not be as pleasant / My fence construct runs / I — I — I — I — I — I — I — I   [ELECTRIC CHARGE]   I — I — I — I — I — I — I /

The fence from "halvah" to thermocline reads something like this

halvah halyard hamate hamey hammerlock hammertoe hammett hammier hammily [...] thermocline thermocoagulation thermoduric thermodynamical thermodynamicist

A thirty second video explaining the process of making a shaving scuttle invades the Institute of Dream Scenario / Reproduction this time is a nightmare that a vase [Greek Style! celebration] is paired with strange cups / Interlocked and dropped / *Let me show you* / and / *It's broken* / Never *It is* in the mind / Ointment **weather** / is an Ointment **Window** / **Condition** / I mean so many **screens** / They are rubbed in all over / Consider it often the ultimate deceit [SCREEN] / —so, what is it hiding? / But, otherwise / To say a condition of poetry is often the poet at the window—at least described scenes (Clark Coolidge, [25] Lyn Hejinian, [26] Cole Swensen, [27]) / This is the evolution of that window from which we watch our world passing by

∩

DISCLAIMER: This book uses many terms which are forbidden or restricted across most social media platforms. Terms such as "killed" are ironically often censored in subtitles on TikTok and such in order to reach a wider audience without these applications and their algorithms censoring their content / [The terms PALESTINE/GAZA/GENOCIDE/SLAUGHTER] / Despite the prevalent State murder of children, women, and men daily the world over, this censorship is persistent within peacetime societies—better: societies at peace—there is no good term for this specious, authoritarian, conditionality [only that peace exists against war]—the frustration obviously that it seems few understand how this represses and suppresses, much like we hide war and violence from children [truth which comes later] in these spaces—rhetorical manipulations of protection of children that are actually a weaponized manipulation by the State to keep you from more widely reacting against it / Censorship is a surveillance technique predicated on anticipating and nullifying the potential for undesired behaviors and activity—replicated in real time in the active censorship of *real* images from Gaza, for instance, on Instagram and other platforms / There are other examples of rhetorical manipulations, such as North Carolina's repeated swindle on women that they are "unsafe" in the bathroom and will be attacked by an ever-shifting cast of villains drawn from the queer and trans communities /

⌒

The letter or email began *Good Morning, David* and mentioned writing in the heat-dome from the stoop in Buffalo. / *Many Americans are aware but comfortable with Global Warming* [—Art Bell loved to quote] / The email did not include discourse, event, or action sequences, learned later—the sequestration of "certain populations" to the West Side which matches the generative pattern in most American cities [see **Kensington Expressway Project** [28] see also **Troost Dividing Line**]. Unmarked vehicles patrol the streets—ICE. The FBI operates **Citizens Academies** in cooperation with ICE and others to instruct and train civilians in raiding homes, surveilling neighbors, and various methods of using and handling weaponry, not to mention manipulation of their communities. This was recently exposed at length in an article in *DocumentedNY*. In Buffalo, at least two iterations of this "Academy" have been held in 2024.

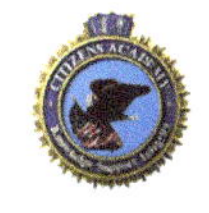

FBI BUFFALO CITIZENS ACADEMY
GUIDELINES FOR NOMINATIONS

The FBI Citizens Academy is a stimulating six- to eight-week program that gives business, religious, civic, and community leaders an inside look at the FBI. During the academy, students gain insight into the structure and operation of FBI field offices and resident agencies and learn the services the FBI provides to local and state law enforcement agencies. It is the goal of the FBI Citizens Academy to foster a greater understanding of the role of federal law enforcement in the community through frank discussion and education.

The next FBI Buffalo Citizens Academy class will be held on Tuesday evenings from March 5 to May 7, 2024--with the exception of April 2 and April 9, 2024--at 1 FBI Plaza, Buffalo, NY 14202.

Nominations for the 2024 class may be submitted by past and/or present FBI employees, Citizens Academy graduates, or any individual wishing to nominate themselves. Individuals nominated must be in good standing in the community.

Candidates must meet the following criteria:

- Be a recognized business, religious, or community leader
- Live and/or work within the division's jurisdiction
- Be at least 21 years old
- Consent to a limited background investigation, to include fingerprint checks
- Agree to attend all sessions, with no more than one excused absence

The copy's indication that Academy candidates *Be a recognized business, religious, or community leader* notes another insidious aspect of the programming: by selecting only local leaders within civic circumstances, the FBI and its partner organizations can implant their agendas and efforts into churches, schools, and places of work in numerous cities with minimal community awareness that this is occurring. Across the nation, while the FBI has long claimed that mosques are hotbeds of radicalization, it is within government-sponsored classrooms that the State's terrorist actions upon vulnerable communities—typically minority, undocumented, and impoverished—are being manufactured, instructed, and perpetuated. While the public school system is already an arm of the State in mandating a propagandized history, [29] alongside the allowances of the military to recruit from high schools, colleges, and so forth, the actual space of the classroom to educate people towards militaristic community surveillance tactics and State-sponsored violences has typically been reserved for military, police, and National Guard operatives within an officiated, differentiated status from the civilian (a status that dictates an authority above my/

our own as civilian). No longer—authority is diminished and altered in order to extend and maintain the State's controls upon the populace. This, then, demonstrates an operation predicated on State concerns towards their potential 'loss of control,' for such juridical escalations—while not unheard of in history—are typically the resultant calculus of societal upheaval and change.

POSTSCRIPT TO THE INTRODUCTION

MAYBE YOU MAKE A BOOK ABOUT THE TARTAN HOLE
/ holes: glimpses into the other text / the text
is full of holes—stretching field, there being entrances
/ the moment [this inception] is a hole / this hole takes
you to another place / in this way it is [the text] similar to
dimensional theories or aspects of the universe as connected
by wormholes to other universes / Maybe it is a book that
is inconsequential / Regardless, terminology is refined
and defined by the subject *at times* / and use of language
concerns or troubles our disputation of the potential for
subjectivity / That was a phrase I read / today *tartan holes*
/ Avant-garde clothiers / their constructions / I cannot
provide an etymology for tartan holes

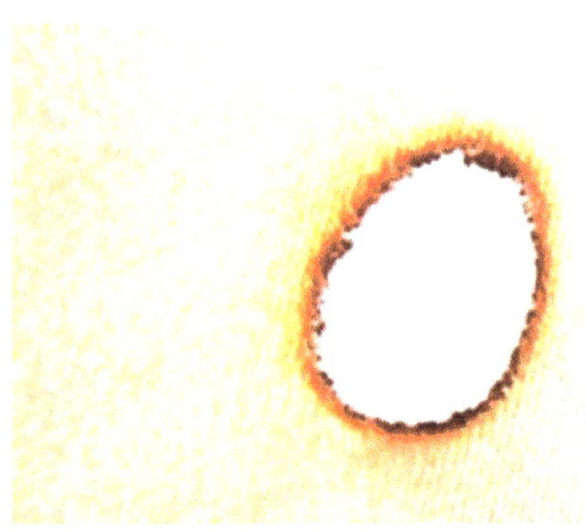

Cigarette burnt silk, a still from Inland Empire (2006)

⌒

Devastated / Shocked / Saddened / These were some of the words I used / But, in reflection, they were all disingenuous / I understood totally

⌒

Asthmatic bladder / There is a request to *Enable dictation* / This means **read back** / "Back" that it was made before / The "asthmatic bladder" is a mishearing that presents a musical "hook" / One imagines it leaks / **Analog: wheezes** / The phone has no hold musak (which is not MySQL despite the phone's insistence to correct) / One wonders, thus, where they are / Work music could be situated across aesthetic pleasures and recognitions /

As a disintegrating tape of The Beatles' "Yesterday" plays / I recall what William Basiniski has noted about the completion of his *Disintegration Loops* / Two towers burn, or is it the gleam of the sun upon them / Smoke—there is no denial

∩

Overhearing / *I have cut many live wires in my life* / and *sometimes, they do bite* / and *It is an awakening experience* / Perfect—three phrases, strung together / They've told me all I think I need to know

∩

Sit down now / to your daily sandwich / that's the promise / in every pot / Skinned alive and / unseasoned / Marijuana capitalism redefines / Store and globular structures / Nationalization on the horizon / We will ensure mandated levels of wheat, chicken, and broth are available

∩

Here is my LAST. Never again. No one reads them! / That's Fanny Howe to Bill Corbett about her novel *Indivisible* at the turn of the millennium / I worry about it / worry over or is it wonder / that turn to an audience / receipt and but / Have yet to even wonder if it is **writing** / *I am not famous anymore* / The nightmare in this reading is / what day will come / when I, too, no longer care / because of the day before / when my back broke because I was ignored

∩

Slash and burn / I hear Joseph is writing about mountain-top removal / **Will you send them to me?** / Friends that keep you informed / Are they informants? / I read from Lyn Hejinian the view that letters are inherently selfish / I agree— / That is a point of comfort / It is okay—we do go on about ourselves / It is then important that we are excited for a receipt / These are acceptable and can be trusted as **facts** from factum—do, action, act, after the act [31] / What is written upon the receipt is therefore constative in nature—this, too, because few of us actually complete the surveys often encoded at their conclusion, meaning the written and, at times, spoken Please complete this survey and tell us about your experience is not articulated in any normative condition where there is an anticipated response. In fact, the authors of such statements are speaking into the rare occasions when someone actually responds and affirms these desires.

If there were a normative condition within that situation, it would be—determinably—one framed by the negative capabilities of an initiated action.

∩

[CRACKLE—URGENT!!!!!!—WIRE CALLING] / Layer cake is analog of generations / It is light and fluffy and it tastes good / Fresh lemon zested into the mix makes it all the better / Dragonflies swarm in the summer garden / The newspaper comes to you by a servant which is a robot / This is the future, when you have dementia, and the newspaper is a tablet / And you are demented, [NARRATIVE PROSE SO FAR, the EDITOR says] so out of time / *Pfhufht* you evaporate what happened to you 80 years ago / Hello, churl / I see you, homing / Radar eyes infrared and sonar equipped / I drone / So, scene set it is [THEATRICAL] [THE PLAY IS NAMED *ANTI-LIBEL*] / [SETTING] Knesset [32]: yesterday (?) / [ENTER] May Golan giving a speech / [SHE SCREAMS] / *I am personally proud of the ruins in Gaza* / She screams to the opposition / *You can keep dreaming we will end the war* / She says *we are not ashamed* / Symbols are destroyed / They are the lies fed / ███████████████████████████ / when she says *Not a dove and not an olive branch, only a sword* / She-Damocles, I warn you "look up" / Golan says she *doesn't care about Gaza* months before / That *they can go out and just swim in the sea* / She wants to see the bodies in the streets of Gaza, but it is obvious we've hardly been there at all / Let alone, and I'd like to see her swim in that sector of the Mediterranean / I imagine her backstrokes with Mao / Mao + May / Where is the silkscreen of May Golan, ironically tucked away in the basement of the former Shah's museum in Iran? / I imagine it feature a prominent red layer— / In 2023, May Golan is appointed by wanted war criminal 'Bibi' to the position of consul-general in New York (e.g. The United Nations) / Israel is formed by an act of the UN the 29th of November, 1947 / On January 26th, 2024, the International Court of Justice—the highest judicial body of the United Nations—announces that *it is plausible that Israel committed genocide in Gaza* but does not call for a cease-fire / The case is primarily brought by South Africa, raging against what they describe as contemporary Apartheid / CHYRON: THIS IS APARTHEID THIS IS GENOCIDE / May Golan on refugees: *Muslim Infiltrators with AIDS blood* / I am a proud racist—May

Golan / ████████████████████████████, Golan must have a domicile in the United States, possibly a hotel paid for by the Israeli government—which makes it more challenging to locate her individual despite the readiness of surveillance her cohort used to execute extrajudicially on a regular basis / I am trying to tell you about the shimmering shield (Have you seen or read *Dune?*) that these individuals have around themselves / It is March 9th, 2024—[clearing throat] good morning and good afternoon / May Golan, you are a murderer / you are a *genocidaire* [33]

∩

I am in an igloo, too / I live there with you / Heavier than metal / That's the suggestion / I align myself in a constellation with E and W forming the shape / I agree with this sentiment / This is the bad spell / I mail things / I did a bad thing(s) / Raptor / Trapper / Hawks swoop in / That's the dark term: swoop—to fell / Squirrels, on branches, to them precipices / Now—it is a live wire / World on the wires / We've built a whole world of wires / And wires are roads / For squirrels and telecomms / And that the squirrel tooth can lethalize what's afoot / Houthi rebels sever a cable in the ocean / The connection is severing

cables, not "animalistic nature" as a fawning reader says—
to that reader, *fuck you* / You do have to be right before you
can get it all wrong / The wrong reading is what someone
else says *look see* / The wrong reading is not the incorrect
reading

⌒

The inevitable result of your return [34] is [will be] **triumph** [35] /
and the form is a car [in my memory] / [EDITORIAL
INTERJECTION: this line fascinates me—can you write an
obituary for [AUTHOR] in prisoner's constraint?]
/ For what it is worth, my friend **tipped off the major
news media that she was dead** / this is esoteric /
T T T T T T H H H H H I I I I I I I I S S I S S S S
is **privately directed** / dictated / I wonder if you are
informed at my stalking behavior / Tracks look like bird
scrawls / What they "left behind" / is **evidence** / [BACK
TO YOU! ☺] / Which is—you are alive / and I am in your
papers / [SO. NOT ☹ (?)] / reading you mention a diary I
also have a copy of / Reading you say you are looking at it /
Reading you experience stomach pain / you take antibiotics
/ You [ME] have an ulcer / Your father denies it for a long
time [BUT "MUMMY" DOES NOT UNDERSTAND

ME] [36] / Then he cuts tumors from under your arm / [I AM MIXING IN MY AUTOBIOGRAPHY] / When you cannot look at it now / And, considering content? / To give it away—an exorcism / [I AM THE EDITOR] / This is a discussion about my research in the [AUTHOR] archive / Your diaries are very sad / Today I read about [WHAT I HAVE ALREADY EXCISED] and request [PRONOUN] letters to you / That's the track of research / I thought I would next need your diaries when [EVENT OCCURED] but / *volta*

Air Words — / I ask you stop vaping / Slipping / Pulling / Down the roads of the parkway that is nighttime and you take naked pictures of me and we walk up and under the apple tree and blow each other / We have our headlights on in this memory, that's the "flash" in our pictures / And then, too, there is the cosmos above / So this comes from the song and what is next / Which is because the song is a memory / So what is next is a dissection of processuality which is my notion of **the work** or what is **production** / I have written elsewhere about Jewel in the Faulkner novel [37] / I am enamored with the crush I had on him in high school / I hear then the soaring aspects to the music which form bridges in my mind / Bridges are the **metonym** / this song uses a didgeridoo / which takes you to "another place" / And N H Pritchard had described, too, "Metognomy" / Second then—next song, and there is a bad thing I did / My husband says *You cannot say that* / My husband guards language? / Moral censer / Oh, I mean *center* / Moral compass / My heart / And in another moment I am compelled to explain my interabled relationship — spoiler alert! Not now but dispersion / The other day my husband woke up different—worse than the day before, in a state of confusion. The next day, he woke up even more confused. The problems are mental and somatic, and the somatic feeds the mental. There is an absolute disarray bodily. He does not regularly defecate, for instance, but only every four days, to his exacerbated issues of gut compaction and such explained by a recent doctor for the hundredth time / while his frequent lack of sleep or fitful rest distributes across many days a confusion or slow activation of the senses, in tandem with a variety of other symptoms, wherein I start my day tuning as he says in my imagination "an engine" that I build up / or make anew / and I also frequently ask *Do you want eggs?* /

Of N H Pritchard, yesterday I read from *The Matrix* and his poem "The Harbour" / So he can split every word, find the perfect vocable, and know how the poem expands a thousand times / This is his form / I am standing near a hallway and

have to lean against the wall reading / It is obvious he "found
a form" / So, reading, I finish this section—I am stunned,
honestly, and my breath runs short it is nerve wracking I
cannot do this

pro   c   l   aimed
s   till   s   i   l   e   n   t

GRIEF SEQUENCE

This time lensed by a dandelion / severed head from the day before adornment / Hollow space below the tree / space where I was mistaken yesterday / Some of us theorize that this is not a strictly flat plane, instead believing in constructions similar to topographical maps / The universe, not a nesting doll / though definitions may appear as such / emerging from each other / and another's incipience / The ducks land "aquatic runways stretching into breadcrumbs" cribbing the imaginative language of childhood stories / rendered to the space of mind at the same time by all the chalk drawings / and all the child signatories / collaborative ephemeral projects / "failing texts" / kite in the sky today, laying on the ground yesterday / The flesh tension—we are pulled in many directions / Sensation—despite the popping sound recently developed in the ear, birds' feathers rustling—methodology of their homing flights / Could the robot reemerge / Destruction of a silent block of women passing / Some people from behind / Natural debris skipping the ground you wonder it is a frog two drops falling at discrete times so inevitably you ask *is it starting to rain* / There again a reminder of the grey / [THEORY SPACE: examining the convenience of rhyme, as it moves sequences and especially so in the production of thinking] / where soon it *washes away*

∩

Suggestion for a poetic sequence replacing pronouns with bracketed lacunae and rendering verbs neutrally to swing between singular and plural situations

∩

Questions arise overnight about a corporation and the potential that they killed a whistleblower / Parts of a fuselage rain over Miami / Let me put it another way, in August of 2009, Dale Hudson was found dead in the PeeDee River, face down. Suspicious circumstances at the scene of the crime alongside a home invasion shortly after at his residence where hard drives and manuscripts were stolen, alongside the information that he was researching organized crime in the area as part of a burgeoning late career turn to true crime writing—interviewing an incarcerated Carolina mobster—

all rule out the accident police hastily determined this to be /
"Mystery" persists around these deaths / questions should be
more accurately framed as forensic audits of the respondent
police departments

⌒

Moment / Child and feels floating / Moment makes **god-
complex** / diary later / moment maybe breeds tears /
Aerotropolis

⌒

The machine says ON / and I hear OFF / what is this
development / CONNECTED / and this keyboard has
adapted a new language / You were to be my sh / grass eater
/ lotus obliterator / not a shoe / my sh / were supposed
to be there / and for six / a sh / not a spool / or a star /
One finds they own no books by Gregory Orr, but several
belonging to him / my sh: my story is different (not even a
variation) / it comes sidereal (pulsations forming shapes)
/ heat death family universe / a dog jumps twelve feet, my
sh—he bit my dog and my hand / bleeding waves, chased
/ In my story, I am not the same age and am myself the
victim of the hunting accident

Gustatory minor—tasting the tones of the keys / one makes

candy pianos / and licorice screens

Grief sequence / rare word from Old French (in this project of the analyzed words) / grever / share grief and grieve / so these move beyond language / which is easy to say / is experience / if the jets fly in the night—as you say, **they, the plural** can only fly in formation, which seems to suggest a militaristic stance, but elsewhere it appears you ride in a jet, so, one wonders it isn't just a very large airport through which you fly over Niagara (elsewise is fantasy and dream of the "other"—as in fantaszied antipodes only somewhat true, as in East and West Coasts) / after time, too, as lines and mappings determine shifts of semantics literally over into landscaping / blending meaning and vision, or sequencing them / Hejinian's "Resistance" features a variety of modes of transport / cars tracking the line sometimes sideways / This release arrives as an envelope informing DO NOT BEND / a scan / an essay / I find the etymological condition more interesting / The etymology of jet / as in jet plane / is especially fascinating

Secondary characters in the landscape, moving / Do you remember the one from before / Who said *I used to be on television?* / So it is not archaeology, it is anthropology /

And now *if any person* / and this one doesn't appear to be able to remember anyone / machine beeping—dying (heart rate monitor—it is / what is beeping) / *There must be a reason it is so clear* / Skyscrapers, and you wonder who mills below them, besides the obvious—their employees / Glass buildings, they are made to resist / made monument eternal / derision of sacred space / and Alice's tapes, buried in the desert, possibly, abandoned to time—we thought there would be more / glitch landscape, full of steel arrays, electric beams arcing between them / and arc is an appropriate term for that situation / Once, [   ] goes they said *you found your form* / that wasn't the first time / seems to be a higher form of praise / an ascertainment / and that is exactly what federal authorities seek to do in registered papers indicating at least a ½ million dollars are owed back over a three year period spanning [████████████] / Mandated homelessness for imbalance, and one had wondered—weapon of the state / they go further when you do not pay / Even where we seek to avoid to pay, say for paying into bombings? / The faultline emerges from their having an authority / Frustrates—*I used to be on television* / where you ignored most of these problems / And when I said [   ] about [   ] I donated [A FEW

THOUSAND] dollars to [Foundation]

as reported to the author by the ever anonymous C— /

Those brackets comically short, just spaces—elisions

∩

§6321. Lien for taxes

If any person liable to pay any tax neglects or refuses to pay the same after demand, the amount (including any interest, additional amount, addition to tax, or assessable penalty, together with any costs that may accrue in addition thereto) shall be a lien in favor of the United States upon all property and rights to property, whether real or personal, belonging to such person.

(Aug. 16, 1954, ch. 736, 68A Stat. 779.)

STATUTORY NOTES AND RELATED SUBSIDIARIES

SHORT TITLE

Pub. L. 89–719, §1(a), Nov. 2, 1966, 80 Stat. 1125, provided that: "This Act [enacting sections 3505, 7425, 7426, and 7810 of this title, amending sections 545, 6322 to 6325, 6331, 6332, 6334, 6335, 6337 to 6339, 6342, 6343, 6502, 6503, 6532, 7402, 7403, 7421, 7424, 7505, 7506, and 7809 of this title, sections 1346, 1402, and 2410 of Title 28, Judiciary and Judicial Procedure, and section 270a of former Title 40, Public Buildings, Property, and Works, redesignating section 7425 as 7427 of this title, and enacting provisions set out as notes under sections 6323 and 7424 of this title, and under section 1346 of Title 28] may be cited as the 'Federal Tax Lien Act of 1966'."

Evidentiary statutes protecting the State in their mandating

homelessness of delinquent payers

∩

Overnight suicide notification / read later / pairs symbolic

bad storms / and went to the barn to sleep with the animals

/ brought the dog with / holding them the entire time / small shaking / and dreams then / elephantiasis, fox masks / Bright flashes the slats / to see stands of trees / and trees only / **stand** is a term oriented to natural resource allocation (later) and should not be perceived to include the mushroom colonies, insects, deer, birds, or even—at times—root systems encountered there the next day or days before

∩

Prawn Jesus / The latest generation / States: We worship the living God Go d of Abram isac and Elijah [sic] / The tools manipulating the images of the State rulers have been revealed [39] / Labeled: untrustworthy / Establishes war tablescape (game playing metaphor) / The one State and the Techno-State / The division between the two broke down long before / relying on un-regulation and systematized one-track thinking

∩

Moving slides / [   ] the school show / and I WON the award / desperate for the attention / of [THE OTHER] / I remember the last time I wore a tie years ago / —an award / I refuse them / Why bother / *they don't give a fuck* / and once, my father beat me till I pissed myself while I was crawling under a bed [EDITOR'S NOTE: the word clamber is more appropriate here] / Triumph / I have realized another form / now back to revise / and leave you behind—you, the fucking **skald**

∩

Fans / etymology of / redaction / *Which is it?* / That's a line of thought of total confusion

∩

Someone is too loud / *The sip of warm champagne is like a sip of butter*

∩

The current trajectory for poor parenting is towards the guillotine—indescribable terrors within the complex / The sights which emerge in your mind / Not those defined by outgoing presidents so much as there was a tv show once called *OZ* / and jokes about soap / and in my head were glassy brick buildings along a mountain slope amidst stands of trees / fog becomes the narrative / rendering a landscape invisible / mist clings—is something you notice when you get off the heath and inside, cooking eggs, sweater wet / That is interesting alongside the futuristic technology subtly included in the novel *Cold Comfort Farm* by Stella Gibbons where video phones and readily available private jet planes are profligate and uncommentated upon / The production of the syncretic text is vital to advancing future discourse upon the storyworld of that farm

⌒

Moving picture / history / Muybridge / to CCTV / exploitation of the animal / exposition of the naked body / time originates as a tracking of discreet imagery, in time moving faster and faster / Periodization as the "Era of the Destruction of the Seams" / belief in no-separation, for instance, is functional diminishment of blinking / To manufacture the world with eyes always open [upon] / With this, the sprawl of narrativization, furthering radial operations of a consistent narrative / With eyes wide open, these producers hope to see a world in meaning / Recording images in and of itself produces interior beliefs (religion) in the moving and still imagery (re-)produced / Suggestive of a superiority, this is it, this is what it was / Marconi dreams have no correspondent structures within photography and videography / However, time travel could be introduced, deploying the body (TRAVELER) with a camera (TECHNOLOGY) to various "outposts" across time (recognizing the impossibility, also, of recording all time and events entirely, considering—critically—the intrusion of the "eyewitness" and such instability of sight or seeing that demand the event be documented from *every angle*—which then expands so the event and tape tracking separate wildly, with some documentations showing the very end, some the very beginning, etc. etc., to track [in other words] the varietal encounter with the event also) so that events could be recorded—were time travel rendered out of theory into possibility / We could bring surveillance technology backwards and 'correct time' / — Marconi's dream is that sound *does not die* but we all know too painfully that the image *does die* / We now understand, also, that sound dies / **Time travel** could also be referred to as **asynchronous teleportation** [40] (which, all teleportation revolves around the transportation of an object or entity from one place to another, which occurs also as one moment in time to another) / *What is a physical qubit / What is a logical qubit / Is a physical qubit in some* *way rendered through particles or matter* / Qubits are *made / If you want to make a qubit* / and with *ions, phosphorous* there are *cubic platforms* / The relative material here is the confirmation of physicality to the otherwise intensely esoteric quantum computing material discussed above—largely not understood by myself or anyone else outside of the field [41] / However, with the knowledge that qubits can be constructed—given that they are made—*To make a qubit—resonator can behave as a qubit—now you have a qubit*—the explanation intensely relies on the largely unexplained term, though the nationality of construction, again, is all that was sought / The **qubit** is a contraction of **quantum bit** / Itself a unit of **information**, and physicality of information is the further reduction of the above, the movement *forward* from here, to then for some reason seek to query a connection between this qubit ideation and the proposed electrical fields of the **mind** as a **computer**, suggesting then an interaction with the quantum mind hypotheses / But, originally, the intentionality of the sequence had been to lead the reader to the concluding line that / *Quantum teleportation has been achieved in numerous experimental situations*

You want to talk about an *obliterator?* / [—devastating—] / Here is the fragmentation of a headline: *embedded in his alter ego* which is absurd! / In the moment, every developmental psychoanalytic theory regarding the impossibility of knowing thyself is erased by the axiomatic command Γνῶθι σεαυτόν and do so so well as to be capable of stepping into the role of an"other"—real or imaginary— empathizing and such with that other role / As an addendum, however, it should be noted that all occupied roles by the *acting* individual (the self) are *imagined* as they are not that other-which-is-a-self / So, the actuality is that these acting selves can readily occupy that "other" space for it exists entirely in the imagination of their selves

What is it that is all around / The world is round / You can get on it and go round and round / The images in *The World is Round* were used by Clement Hurd as wallpaper and carpet in his own home [42]/ We never have good seats, but opera glasses reveal an audience and one wonders, listening to this—this appears to be fabulation [43] and one wonders, one wonders the price of memory is the price of an advance

/ Still, the work is viable or capable of commiseration / Reproductions of reality in viability systems rely on associations along class lines / Many of us have determined we are not interested in material texts articulated or under the throes of the productive concerns of the classes we do not belong to—shamefully when the class below us and artfully when the class above us / Capsule of life—association along *similar lines* which is to derision and the "wrong fit" in favor of / in lieu of a vertical reading—so the general experience is horizontal and the affliction is a disease of horizontality / I, too, have hyperhidrosis which is particularly problematic during my working hours of 7am to 11am

ANTITRUST

A CIVIL POETICS FROM A(RT) TO G(OOGLE)

I now "reject" the viability of erasure poetry in the wake of the SCOTUS ruling on Warhol and Fair Use [44]/ Perhaps, I *should* be greatly concerned / Perhaps I should grab the safe and the music box, then run / I've done it before

∩

We will live like they do / We will hold the egg / our arms splayed a cross and back to you / We will stand and pose / We will pick on you / We will remove verbs from the air and direct them at you / We will write stories / as I read, We ask thoughtful questions and cry / you say, *We are a poem* / no form We produce what / articulation We / journal We / talent We / favored We / will, live like they do / We do, Will, live like they do / they call We / make fun say or maybe wonder are We / detached and with no interest and interested in the use of an algorithm to compare this with that text / Confusion setting in after ECT so I spend the first hours of the afternoon reminding [█████████] about the day before and the morning of / Loss [Glazier] writes [to me in an email] that "late work" as a project does make sense though to note his association with Transcendental Meditation asserts that his work now (phenomenologically "late") is **present work** / and of course it is and I have not mentioned to him / to cripple thus demand him say thus / there is **late work** and with being a young reader [ME NOW] there is **working backwards** / and between these, there is a bringing to the foreground of a thread—not spooled around an odradek / [   ] hated or hates—complex given he is dead— [MY FATHER] / the syncretic space is to breathe p r e s e n c e / it is applied all over me / sunscreen / says the title interjected here

⌒

As another mark against sound, the issue of harmonization / Within visual perception, harmony is a sensation of a complete picture, perhaps, but, save for passing screens such as people, cars, or jets occupying a moving trajectory across the plane of sight, most objects remain static and visible, or, more readily, discernible [being there the need to state **visible** and **vision** as or away in terms of their "actionality" from **discernible** and **discern**: in **visioning** the world, one is merely having eyes or ocular capacities, the **discerner** makes sense of the visual space before them [45]] / Not exactly etymological save the explication of the bifurcation / Sonically, the issue is much different, despite the mere space of inches between the eyes and ears, and the shared processual organ through which sensory information in these veins is assessed and re-produced in conscious thought / A sound can overtake another one / When my husband is playing a video game while I use the speaker, and I realize the low-volume soundtrack isn't tracking in my mind, having been overtaken by the similar sonic structures emanating from the speaker—which is a collaborative release by Brian Eno, Roedilius, and Moebius, while my husband is playing Mario Kart / The conclusive image—rendered abstractly—is seen discreetly: red hands triumph in a fast momentum along the floor of the cave (there appears to be no particular geologic term describing these types of naturally-occurring floors versus

manmade floors, opening the definitional space to the same
potential confusion that arose when being instructed that
piso era la base de la habitación y al mismo tiempo era
todo el apartamento o habitación o vivienda en sí)

∩

Site Visit

Start below / in gardens / there is an idea about watching
someone and realizing that process is trial and error—
there are no defined grand lessons remembered when it is
all set aside for years—though some trials destabilize the
chain and force you to the side of the road to work on your
bicycle until you can ride it again, if at all (trial and error,
also—self-repair) / But, then went elsewhere, avoiding the
gardens / Response≠static: this air [I do not forget] and
day [the earth I tread], mixture of response so some in wool
and coats while others in no shirt or shirt and shorts, the
runners moving smoothly and water reflecting too brightly
the sun on the eyes, so avoiding the lakeside—not admiring
water / When attempting to discern bark examples across
medieval paintings, one is best advised to note that these
are rarely scientifically informed / The sign advertises a
Mineral Wall → / Inside and outside the museum adjacent

to this sign in the parking lot of a building of KCAI is Andy Goldsworthy's monumental sculpture *Walking Wall* / This is another gallery day—although here I am, in the heating-up car, interpreting / There was another statement about those paintings I wanted to make, which related there being *just a tree* to the essential figure from Sassure, wherein it really cut aside the matter that the word **tree** "describes nothing"—in these works

árbol arbor árbore arbre árvore дърво дрэва дрво

are perfect renderings of the (ap)perceived "real thing" / Aspects of museums often overlooked, especially larger "complex" ones—physical plants are necessary / In this instance, a limestone smokestack with neutral carvings emblamatizes a disgust held towards the industrial— of which, minimal representations, if at all, of brutalist artworks are exhibited herein (the work *Lichtfalle* may be an exception, although critics and scholars pinpoint Anselm Kiefer's work as within the superstructural neologism "neo-expressionism" / Car horn lows / *What the fuck bitch* / and the cyclist screaming—suddenly it narrativizes the sequence of events before I [████████] and walk

inside / Every army is headless—that's the co-option
of a citizenry by the State force rendering all subjects
anonymous commodities—consider then also wars of
attrition and helicopters hovering over cities / Helicopters
provide the soundtrack to day-to-day life (believed to be
stasis—as in hiding—) in Port-au-Prince watching the
violent spiral without intervention—only evacuating the
wealthy / A line of children wait to board a bus outside
the Bloch Building / On the stairs, above in the porticos,
opaque screens of glass occlude vision for no explicable
reason—it is "the nice neighborhood" in the city—this
(not the buildings we are crossing through now) was once
a mansion and estate, and is notable [for a large museum]
as one whose founder merely left a massive endowment for
the free collection (amalgamation) of art, creating a sort
of encyclopedia / Encoded in a line or yellow dress, in a
room with a hanging vine creeping / The way rooms are
badly designed / Here is MC [46] from "The Contemporary
Figure" that *Art history seldom elevated works of art that
feature people of color or their stories* just so that if you go
to the other wing of this museum, you will find that Art
Historical perspective also seldom include reckonings of
bigotry in previous generations of art productions

—this is what the gallery attendant tells the child in the room adjacent to the one I was just speaking of—there is a family activity and docent available in the abstract expressionist room, explaining and jovially imparting the joy of aesthetic experiences. The same is not true for the adjacent room where is "The Contemporary Figure" / *I see two stick figures*—something so absurd overheard someone adjacent laughs, and much attention is paid to decoding a Pollock / Technicolor dream coat shifted into the situational out of the disco or jazz era, and the overlay of geometry—this is a better perception in the moment of what is happening / The word-processor acts up—you cannot just hit it on the side / *Abstract—you can just move the pieces around*—so it is incoherent information, coming in clipping / though every work has its un-work / the system autocorrects the name of every artist in the exhibit / *Did you think you were going to learn about art today? Every Saturday, from 1-4* / The escape logic or route in this scenario—the horn blows / or through the horn blowing then see the crowd in black robes gathered / The discretionary moment, avoiding the surveilling eye / And, to begin to notate moments of surveillance—it could be only just a window, or, it could be the silkscreening of film prints—the perceived thing seen on screen / Someone looking back at you—but then the overlaying neon refractory glazing / Screen and sieve—made things / *Stella, is this synonymous of light* (especially—metallic) / Your tone merges with that tone—color theoretical space of a third consideration about above concerns towards discernment / Photorealism accelerates and diminishes along a spectrum of proximization / Merger—then the thought that this could be viewed also apparently from a balcony that one has not noticed before—merger / Merger of wood and granite, as well as manipulation, where the wood is cut, along the cut lines into the granite, and then also that the object is set (and is **the object** a **machine**—consider) underneath warm lighting so that it has a sort of glow on some verticals / *THE SOUL HAS MORE NEED OF THE IDEAL THAN OF THE REAL* / **(End Site Visit)**

Website Visit

The machine indicated originally that that line there about the soul was in Comfortaa / Suggesting, then, a brief tribunal [in other words **the time has come**] / As evidence, then, presented: [each is a **CASE** which buried as definition in *OED* there but is more readily apparent when regarding V "n1" of **Docket**]

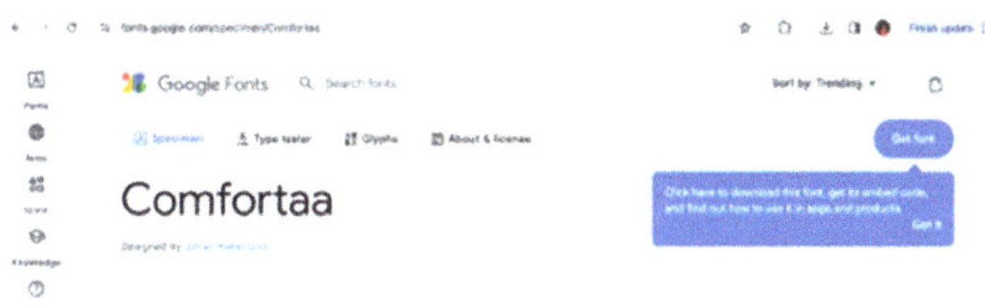

Google Fonts webpage advertising Comfortaa to users, noting attribution to the creator

Whereas a common understanding of these rights and freedoms is

No one shall be held in slavery or servitude; slavery and the slave trade shall be prohibited in all their forms.

Additional copy from the same webpage

It is obvious to wonder *What are these encoded messages?* / Notating the heavier weight to the one side, and the lighter weight to the other—that this is not entirely about making space and graphic design, but to then highlight the keyword and phrase, which is **common** and **whereas a common understanding** so that this is an if-then construction, the corporate being the *then* and there being the need to advance the corrective *which will come later*—is the horizon of *now* / [EDITOR'S NOTE: beware corporate readings, which are technological] / The creator of the font is inspired after watching a documentary on the commoner, **Helvetica** / He just wanted—at the time—for a *softer* font than the NLA [Century Gothic] [47] / so it is **comfortable** as point of [etymological] origin / And—for those confused readers mistaking the corporate copy with Constitutional Rights "afforded in the 14th Amendment" by the United States of America's Federal system—be aware that the copy is instead from the much-later [rhetorically flawed] "Universal Declaration of Human Rights" which explicitly does not warrant the rights therein to amalgamate bodies of capital generation (the corporation), but instead only the human

/ Google itself reveals the rationale for the deployment of this (public domain fair use in the commons) document as an extension of its marketing page, found at https://about.google/human-rights/ / [48] / Google's notation of their due diligence towards this cause begins with the statement that *We incorporate civil and human rights principles into Google's long-term strategies and day-to-day decision-making* / and continues to acknowledge that they seek *external engagement* with *affected stakeholders* / Only 4 - 5 % of Google's employees in the United States (in sectors of leadership and engineering software development) appear to be Black citizens / roughly half of the employees in engineering and software development are registered to be of various Asian diasporic descent or immigrant status / Google itself publishes less clear, though revealing reporting of its diversity 'targets' annually, wherein is the following chart (effectively rendered in **corporate language**, e.g. utilizing the house codes of Roboto font and pleasantly curved lines:

Hiring by race / ethnicity

The following factors must then be considered:

1. the racial makeup of Asian and Black Americans is as follows in the United States per the Census Bureau: 13.6% Black, 6.3% Asian

2. Google's hiring practices are clearly discriminatory and preferential and regard a disturbingly public acknowledgment of the same when in published materials

3. The data from Google, in 2022, was described elsewhere in that report as being representative of the company's *Best year for hiring* [. . .] *Black+ employees*

4. Per the same report, Google only implemented racial equity initiatives for its black employees in 2020

Advancing from a [publicly held] human rights perspective [49] considering that—tracking issues of rights and their accessions by oppressed groups—typically racial groups are able to earn a semblance of rights or personhood before the law and institution prior to sexualized minority groups [as in the implementation of the Civil Rights Act and the overturn of *Lawrence v Texas,* and the situation faced by the transgender community now legislatively [50]], the report notes that Google implemented extensive efforts towards those sexually minoritized groups prior to the racially minoritized group of their own design [51] / It is easy enough to capture and promote the situation of the most-current crisis, while acting as though an ongoing one in tandem with it (the superstructure is hatred) is resolved *enough* / So, you need a reminder—which is State violence against the unliberated group, the group you both ignored and predatorily targeted wherein it aligned to some esoteric algorithm of neoliberally predicated "DEI" computations [52]

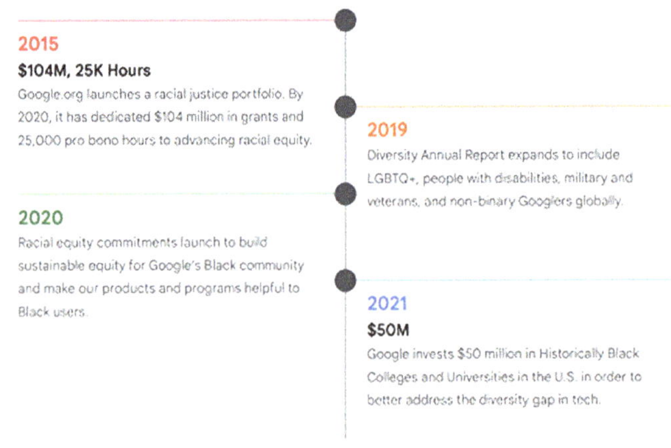

As with many mega-corporations developed in the United States, Google has found it methodologically easier to **outsource** racial equity within the Black community, as indicated in an audit of the corporation conducted in 2022-23 by WilmerHale:

> *In 2020, Alphabet [53] committed to investing $100 million in Black-led startups and venture capital firms in an effort to expand access to capital for Black founders and funders. By the end of 2022, a cross-functional group of Alphabet companies had deployed the entirety of those funds and provided training, technology, and advice to recipients.*

It is unclear the total cost of hiring a substantial cohort of Black Americans to create racial parity in their employee pool, however, it is presumably far higher than the offset costs occurring here in the external investments—the reality of the situation is that such investment casts a pall over the corporation's hiring practices, wherein such investments go far beyond infrastructural development and education, and to further recognize talent and capacity in individual and group entrepreneurial communities created by Black Americans—these investments leave one wondering why the demographic ratios of employees at Google do not align more with the Census Bureau's—and then to conclude the tribunal with the verdict or proclamation that

We call then for mandates, quotas, and extensions of legislative affirmations to guarantee that no private or public organization can manipulate their ranks to exclude a reasonable grouping along racial lines equitable to reality—such is to also then say avoiding such or decrying such, then to go and fix the problems with why people are not wanted, to say *we only want the most able or capable* is to outright acknowledge the systemic issues overall that have left such parties out all along

/ 54

PHOTO | STREAM | SCROLL

work / instead remember when we'd go from one job down a few blocks to the burger hop to score / Get fixed up on the way back to work / The boss calls you in / to her office, for what timeth this is? / Accuses you of— / But, lately, the "frequency" (T quotes T quoting B about CC) has been nocturnal / Four hours in, and I shrug off— no sleep / Looking for better reception / Mornings have produced extensive combat with hyperhidrosis of the hands, prompting you to buy gloves in order to continue basic research tasks on the book / Just as these pages from the spirit duplicator have long been guarded from the sun, now they must be defended—along with shoes—from sweating of the palms (and feet—[EDITOR'S NOTE: Clear this up—reads as you walking on books]) / ULINE offers lightweight models beginning at a dozen for 7$ and the recommendation is that these be worn for the maximal amount of time to counteract the inevitable cost deficits incurred by this medical development, considering that your line of work by force demands your own hands interact with manuscripts, letters, bills, contracts, mimeo pamphlets, first editions, broadsides, and other publications and papers all too ready to register the tactile encounter / Just there, a thumbprint / The day the *Supplemental Poems* arrive, and I'm cooking, and you show it to me—I barely touch it a second and the paper cover draws the oil from the brushing-past finger / A mark, a stain, inflicted on paper

⌒

What do Jena Osman's *Motion Studies,* Julio Cortozar's *Fantomas,* and Jalal Toufic's *Vampires* have in common? If you only look at issues of **motion**, Osman's work bridges between the two, being more full of (loco)motion, while the morpheme "motion" appears more often in form as **motionless** in *Vampires* and [**alt-def:** synonym synonym] **stasis** cum **manipulation** is the ambulatory sensation in this rendering of *Fantomas* wherein the globalist villain prevents freedom of movement by the (oppressed) polis, itself a recurrent theme for instance in *Motion Studies* such as on pages 29-30, where it is written of **ankle bracelets** that *When the signal is broken, they* [THE POLICE AS FORCE-ARM OF THE FEDERAL

STATE] **move** *in and make an* **arrest**. / One then immediately noted the editorial addition (here) of boldface to accentuate Osman's text—**move:** desde movere (move, stir, agitate, upset, disturb) et(y(&)) arrest: ad- & restore (to + remain, continue, stop, sit, stay) / Arrest, being the other acting upon the subject, logically derives from explicit commands, as to train a dog to stop, to sit, to stay

⌒

On broadsides, Allison Hull writes *A broadside is merely a piece of paper with a message on it. A poetry broadside is so much more.* / One wonders the difference, appending "poetry" to the category as something that opens a space for more / and I see two friends have broadsides through Hull's workshop, Joseph and Bruce / Sometimes, these woodcuts grace the body of the poem / Sometimes they stand aside / The latter is the typicality / More's etymology runs / māra meer mehr (and not *māra meet Nehru,* as the machine corrects) / Māra was the temptor of Buddha / the devil analogue that offers more / after taking sociology asynchronously online, one is mocked for mispronouncing "mores" by a friend who then describes their in-person experience at a community college in the same course (different institution, same course prefix)—where, in one experiment, she wore a collar and leash and was "walked" through a mall, an event that has since been completely erased from her memory and all potential discussion despite the intensity and variety of the public response to this "incident" (her reflexive description), which one then wonders about the multitude of (surveillances) recordings of this that must exist—untethered to *her* name but featuring her *body*—across the internet / In *Motion Studies*, Jena Osman tracks the development of CCTV, noting not only the shift from private to public markets of this technology but that for sake of preserving future space, *To save storage space, only one of every six seconds are recorded, a stuttering recounting.* [55] / As tonic to Hull's poetry-centric definition, the exhaustive scope of the Library of Congress features this copy *Essential late-breaking news was transmitted as broadside "Postscripts" or "Extras" to the weekly newspapers.* / Hull's poetic choices explain her definition—none of the broadsides from her workshop announce any "news" / Joseph replies to my note about his father's hat / He's in Boone, NC / TY, I'm reading Frank O'Hara

and working on a poem about him in E News and
sending love. JB / Totally abashed and smiling, [56] I
begin my reply

⌒

Simultaneous perceiving / one man rule extension /
burn after reading—*we will read then burn the incensed
paper* / Strikes then to put to paper / Extension versus
ephemerum / Marconi dream recurs—wondering what
if the dream were to hear *Sònjàdà* performed etc. / Lives
before the **cylinder reel tape vinyl compact-disk
mp3 .wav** / .wav has no etymology being a contraction
/ Reel, however, fascinates, being from "oldest" time [of
the language] hreol [57] / You can hear it / it echoes the
Odradek

⌒

Dismal / Invent an epigraph / black cat lookdown /
lookout—hiking memory relayed to a friend / the jump /
down floor / the chase / up stairs / hours in a day / filtration
system / new economy / the difference / too many people
/ mouths to feed / too much / will we still / will we still
watch tv / will we still go to PE / will we still eat / will

we still / When you walk into the room, you realize what we are doing, though the image was not readily viable for you prior to that walk-in / At the same time, memories of the author's high school architecture come back to them viscerally for the first time in 10 years, and doing so, clearly—there was a love of breezeways

∩

[EDITOR'S NOTE: readers need to understand that the loss of **Verdana** is only the result of the contributions **Trebuchet** afforded the text]

∩

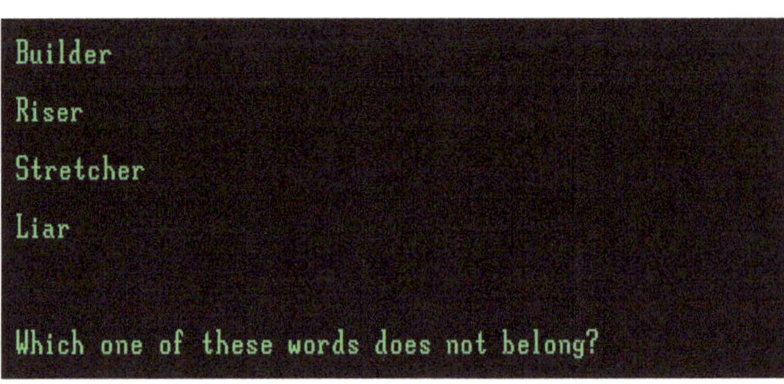

∩

I quit / and *Why'd you quit* / or *did you quit?* / are frequently paired questions / It is all too easy to forget that within the specular situation of our own jobs, our perspectives, disgruntling, and biases towards those not within our field (those outside our jobs) are behaving in this or that way, uninformed by our labor / In this instance, relationally, a non-profit has a technological issue for one of its fundraising websites / Instead of acknowledging the technological issue, [███████████ [██████]] doubles and triples down on this "workplace lens-bias" being theorized, deploying [██████████ [████████]] disdain towards "the donor class" repeatedly in response to [THE AUTHOR] raising the technological concerns directed to them from their mother, sister, and several friends (those friends who did not outright refuse to support [█████████ [████ █████]]) / Non-profits often hide behind their not for profit status, which valorizes a movement against capitalist drives / I can name two non-profits in North Carolina— one medical and one political—that have employed an avowed white supremacist (who identifies as a gay man) who enjoys to annotate and mail copies of Eustace Mullins pamphlets in the mail / His was a conservative upbringing down the line of the family tobacco farm / His father a Republican organizer / The media franchises spawned from the graphic novel (comic series) *Watchmen* includes the television series *Watchmen* / Viewers should anticipate, when regarding literary technique, the "reveal" or "shock twist" in the character played by Don Johnson (a White sheriff sympathetic and cooperative with Black colleagues and neighbors). Considering the media's deployment of the ever evocative maxim *Quis custodiet ipsos custodes*, it is no surprise to find the "watchman" enjoying his position of power as a means to actively participate in insidious white supremacist activities / The previous man in question is actively involved in "liberal" political organizing / The get-out-the vote movement is currently being heavily attacked in progressive camps as the vanguard of maintaining the neoliberal status-quo (and, for instance, platforming Joe Biden and Kamala Harris to enable and arm the genocide in Gaza) / Some weapons only function after benignly going inside the enemy lines, unperceived [58] / There is no oversight or management to prevent these issues from emerging in the public / We vote or we watch /

⌒

Mark / Spring / Difference / [That person—sinecure] / The flag spins wildly around the pole, causing a pulsing of the light behind it as it revolves—one wonders that wind isn't coming from the ground directly below / solar winds bearing companion earthly wind—perhaps borne from hell, so there are solar and ice winds—scenes where you see winds, as over the glaciated landscape [Antarctic research station] / Mark spring's difference—burst away the isolation / Mixed weather, and cold days felt different—what you mean is you hear children playing outside (their screams) even though it is sub-freezing and the wind is visible

∩

Gut the voice / guttural / donation / *down* treat *down* treat / *reading opens doors* / Large groups intercede with each other, causing conflict that is not handled properly

∩

There is a movement / says between then and now / says the clucking of a hen / the barn—the fox slaughter the morning we wake up, that is *another then*—a memory in ▮▮▮▮▮, the landscape feature / In this one, between generations or better yet eras / Maybe, then, that music was better / There is an admiration *now* for nostalgia / launched in vapor bottles some prefer it injected in clear tubes—a gas flowing / The analogy that is easiest is the combustion engine / In 2024, Hertz fires its fifth CEO in four years, and sells ⅓ (20,000 vehicles) of its electric car fleet—the reasoning for the firing? Hertz "bet" on the electric car industry / Alan Ruck cannot explain the cause of the accident he appears to have "led" in his brand new Rivian Truck—a technology authorities speculate he was unfamiliar (and thus somehow "fiddling") with when the accident(s) occurred / Netflix additionally bets on fears of vehicles produced, for instance, by Tesla when capturing a sequence in a recent film [EDITOR'S NOTE: the author assures this is intentionally unnamed despite their additional assurance they watched the film in full and found it middling] / Julia Roberts wanders a slowly emergent—(alt-defs: newly emergent. ruptured. etc etymologies examining "emergent" and "ruptured" which would be then "emerge" and "rupture" look as thus—not knowing if there is a connection: ex (et) e + mergere which is rendered as *to dip out* in an appeal from across millenia to the youth of a certain time around now—while processing forward, and not proceeding, rumpere (et) ruptura which are "to break" which in what sense does dipping break something?—electronic and digital at least, therein the connection being some sort of **portention** wherein in this instance the word actually is **omenous** or **ominous**) / The slow dog joins me and examines the work, their examination being a pressure upon my left arm altering my methodology for typing to accommodate their presence—regardless the autonomous nature of surveillance, the alteration of action as is the impact on the subject by the object (acting inherently as a SUBJECT) occurs / **Julia Roberts wanders a newly emergent dystopian American landscape**—anticipating the "possible blockbuster" of Alex Garland's forthcoming *Civil War* which will show (showed) comparable despairing imagery of the imperialist United States in decay and rapid dismantlement [EDITOR'S NOTE: one wonders if you could poetically utilize the word **disarmament** instead of your choice of diction, at this point, in order to advance a further lensing of political or globalized critique? Considering also the spectral violence such massive weaponry evokes to people outside the immediate landscape, for instance by ecological impact or **ecocide** to the point to also then note that these **residual**

effects or impacts you perceive may come later are actually the now-happening effects of climate change on the various communities you are not part of the world over, starting, for one, in the Sundarbans] / Julia Roberts wanders a rupterous [EDITOR'S NOTE: **ruptureous?**] street where Teslas come in crashing one on the other preprogrammed to congest the artery of what was once a parkway and has become overnight an escape route—cut off / The escalating criticisms by witnesses of the film do very little to enter into the space of imagination of "what if it happened here" which is epithetic in its being profligate—so often utilized as argumentation in concept, but when presented through multi-million dollar convincing special-effects (CGI) the audience yawns and turns away / There is similar minimal viewership of films about Palestinian experiences, as well as such examples as *The Syrian Bride* despite their immediacy and effective *poietical* hybridity in **documenting** and **navigating** and **mediating** the day-to-day experience of what is your and my life / When the last sounds come in, the instrumental avoidance is to say that *this is pleasant* which is the effect of any brass section generally—alongside grandeur / What remains is the varietal recognition across societies of horns as harbingers—most likely through their inevitable use on wide battlefields, where they indeed acted AS SUCH / The horn manifests across time and culture as music of the apocalypse

MEDIUMSHIP

In a moment / the object becomes a totem / with the laying of hands / you lay your hands on the book / with the laying of hands / the object becomes a totem / in a moment

⌒

Stand on the ground / move / feel / look at the sun for citation / and deny the feeling / proceed confined—in a lie or lies / lying or laying of lines / lines in the sand / sand is ground / cloud cover amasses / covered sun / *I will not cross*

⌒

Alternative could be—moonlight coverture / refractional movement moment / breathe contracted, watching / lines of geriatric humans slowly dancing / is a formation / arms gracing an arc up, an inward turn along the rest / now, hands orient to the moon

⌒

Galatea / *born for* (or, from) *me* / emblem

⌒

Slide show: the first slide / *I think I will incorporate slides* is the mentality Susan Howe has in the Denver diary from 1993, seemingly having not used slides before—and, upon traveling to Berkeley to present said talk, she misplaces at least one slide, and feels foolish for what is left out (the situation being that no one but her knows the excision, but it "ruins" the event for everyone within this space—riddled with authority) / So, the first slide is of a chicken nugget in a training video—he, being a gendered caricature made of upholstery, is dipped in barbecue sauce, changes shape, and twirls a lassoed whip above his head where sits a ten gallon hat / The next slide—presented by an indiscernible entity talking—shows a celebrity chef and four children, the chef having taken a chicken carcass of minimal flesh and lots of bones, and blended it in a food processor [EDITOR' S NOTE: that **processed** could have been a more appropriate word choice in this instance] makes the chicken nugget from the first slide, representing the abysmal nutritional content. While the children are disgusted, none of them would pass up the opportunity to eat the freshly prepared chicken nugget / The Smithsonian Museum of American History claims to have the first gold nugget on display that caused the Gold Rush / Careful consideration of the MC for this display shows that the nugget is only *believed to be the first piece of gold discovered in 1848 at Sutter's Mill*

∩

The book of a thousand books is not an encyclopedia but an autobiography (?)

∩

Motionless dead herald an atheistic text—there is no reflection or ideation towards, for instance, the transmigration of "the soul" from "this plane" to "that one"—no psychopomp circus flight, no ET over the sky—going "home" / *Motionless*—so we remain / Landlocked or sinfully terrestrial / Toufic's vampires *regain animation* [59] / regagner / the French choking back into "this" life / Is this second life or Act II / What is the nature of the return / / the 9/11 dead are used in the opening of *Zero Dark Thirty* and as backbone to the composition *On the Transmigration of Souls* by John Adams— *missing. missing. missing.* / In the years since, the composition remains static, not updated to reflect what has been found or regained / Someone writes a thank you note to an Ebay seller for the high quality used VHS player they ordered, noting how they watched home video tapes for the first time in decades, seeing their retirement, seeing their wedding / *Many of those faces are no longer around* / When replaying the audio track, it **recurs** or **runs back** to you / The same feeling appears to occur in the VHS viewer, though dead souls are only illusions regarded, and not interacted with / **Animate** as solvent **anima + animare + animat** / Points of **life** / A new manual has been released for the construction of homes, which controversially suggests (mandates/dictates) that all dwellings be one story affairs

∩

I call on the war cabinet, the chief of staff and the general of the northern command to **come to their senses** *and transfer the war to the enemy's territory* [60] / The human is typically associated with five senses (sight, hearing, touch, smell, taste) / Some postulate proprioception as a sixth sense— the body in alignment with space (the world) / Many autistic individuals experience differences in sensory processing and perception / Induced autism is a factor explored by Shaun Gallagher in the article "The cruel and unusual phenomenology of solitary confinement" /

The critical statement in the article, regarding the term "induced autism" (as correlated to the changes incurred during solitary confinement), reads thus

> *Prisoners who are subjected to solitary confinement show symptoms and describe a phenomenology that is not equivalent to either autism or induced autism, but reflect similar motor problems, and often times more extensive and serious disruptions of experience.*

Psychosocial studies of children to determine post-birth induction or exacerbation of autism in children are rare, though increasing—these studies being separate from false allegations of vaccine-induced autism / The basis of these ideas in Gallagher's work as well as more broadly (Spectrum News) is a study on Romanian children orphaned during the late stages of the dictatorship in the 1980s / Deprivations in these situations permanently alter human experiential behaviors and thoughts / Another example could be the character of "Red" in the ███ show *Orange is the New Black*, whose character arc suggests a difference from "induced autism" towards the space of Gallagher's article (the *more extensive and serious* of his comment)—dementia / Dementia, a degenerative sensory and cognitive disordering of the subject's mind, appears as exacerbated by social isolation in her story, while likely developing naturally regardless—the social conditions of her prison sentence deprive her ability to experience a "normative" life upon release (which does not occur) as the psychosomatic changes to her/the subject in the prison system have destroyed the prior subjectivity experienced / Glib comments are routinely made when tragic or graphic crimes occur demanding the perpetrator be strung up or raped by fellow inmates—*they'll get theirs* the polis screams / A formula develops showing ignorance of statistical data and recent published studies on subject-condition alteration by prison's alongside the polis' rhetoric—the solution is a space outside of the State, which is then co-opted by State agents to further dismantle the notional structures of innoncence until proven guilt / cognitive dissonance manifests at times as "tone-deafness" and denial, but is brought on by psychological stress related to environmental conditions and traumas, such as holding a phone and reading about child murder or rape / empathy is not a sense, but an emotion / sense experience feel

emote are all alterable factors of cognition or perception that conditions of the environment impair or enhance / Recent weather conditions: pandemic, invasions, genocide

⌒

As an addendum, additional sympathetic synonyms: privilege is an experiential social condition which shapes sensory and experiential perceiving / There is then subject-subject or subject-object interaction, along with a universe of positive and negative examples (terms of potential) for furthering discussion / apparatus articulations and advanced anomalies / the *you can do this* affordance

⌒

How much money do the propagandists pay to enter into our timelines (*their timelines can be bought for*) / A flurry of articles in 2013 report Israel as a haven for advertising funding for companies such as Facebook (now Meta) and Google, who were taking in NIS500million or more, equivalent to NIS572,369,293.84 in 2024–USD155,880,094.23 at that time, a figure which has since doubled, and tripled (though not the notorious triple-of-the-doubling) / The origin point for my question was the replacement of AI Christ imagery (the fuselage+half of Christ="beautiful cabin crew Scarlett Johansson") with blatant propaganda for Israel—a country whose actions and ideology I do not support just as much as I do not support my own country of citizenship—I see not patriotic content (Dodie Bellamy posts to Instagram March 18th, 2024 *Should I feel bad?* [A: No, you shouldn't] with a screenshot of an unsubscribe notification email for Joe Biden's 2024 presidential campaign) and have done my best to evade the United States political advertising apparatus (typically a corporation funding advertisements in lieu of them being for the time being blocked from as a business entity donating to the candidate in question—a donation in kind, or so I thought, but according to the law, I am totally incorrect. Currently, allegations about Joseph Biden's son receiving funds, alongside his brother and sister, from Chinese banks and companies, has focused on foreign interference in government—buying influence. Were the law otherwise, however, one could "follow the money" from one country into the campaign coffers of a candidate in another) / picking up wherever the grammar breakdown occurred—there is an exertion against my keystrokes logged into the algorithm that has presented a need to brainwash me, thus activating this line of advertisement in hopes I will be persuaded / While we seek to avoid landing on a final line, we cannot resist / but to offer the hope that *We will not* [61]

⌒

Title connections / Craigslist MC / *I miss you* or *I miss sixteen* / The closer year I had a [   ] : to my head or in my hand / fifteen is not sixteen, while the space between them gets wider as integers pack in behind the decimal / Every number is capable of division into infinite parts, though normative digits are still expected to move forward one by one regardless the destabilizing nature of this information / At the same time, no one inscribes $5.\infty$ in answering any word problem / Sally is studying drone strikes in a 10-minute period and finds that there were 6 drone strikes during that time, resulting in a total of 32 casualties. What is the average casualty count per drone strike during this 10-minute period?

⌒

Nearly a billion Indians will elect their next government in a seven-phase election that starts on April 19 and ends with the declaration of results on June 4. [62] / Over the six years from 2017-23, the Indian Supreme Court determined that voting was not a fundamental right, but a human choice—voting would thus not be rendered compulsory / As with many "democratic" systems, India's non-compulsory voting laws create a gap between **registered** and **actual** voters with around 910 million registered voters in the 2019 election cycle, with a reported turnout of 67%—roughly 609 million voters / The leadership vote itself was far lower—roughly one half of the overall turnout voted for either Narendra Modi or Rahul Ghandi / The article in question commencing this portion details Ghandi's INDIA coalition as primary opposition to Modism in 2024 / Three years ago, my next door neighbors car had a sticker of Modi—of all places—on its sunroof, a very large decal—underneath the portrait, MODI FOREVER / Abki baar, Trump Sarkar—Narendra Modi, Houston 2019 / This time it's the turn of / The lady's not for turning / *Oh—those lights were brutal. They come from the dishonest press? Don't turn them off,* [...] *don't turn them on—don't turn the lights on* / Excuse me, my turn

⌒

Process is one thing, **development** is another

SINTHOME | SEHOMEME | SEHOMYTH

An alternative to the title / Looking for myself in different places / Something simple, manageable and concise / But there is an issue in representation—a reliance on the audience to a greater end than is possible / So confusion erupts against celerity of thought / But, you still managed to get all the right words in

⌒

How it happened was that you went to an event / Which requires you board a plane, then a second plane, in order to get there: a) the event b) a job c) a needed separation d) a free ride? / At the event—**alt-def: conference** or **symposium** / Surroundings of alterity—trimmings along the wall are even different than *here* / Some wallpapers have a sort of satin finish and texture to them, plump and soft, which make certain rooms more ideal for leaning in

⌒

Amongst an **alterior** motive / Meditations unfurl in different directions than the original telos / Call this a swerve **alt-def: clinamen** / (though not so enamored with aleatoric procedures) / [63] / Clinamen as necessitated term / *We have to explain our change* / —and seeks to do so here **documenta** / First came the fall of matter (atomism) as rain—even threads descending from the sky or cosmos or metempsychosis / This stage felt so **predictable**, but in reality was more so **superficial**, prediction being the observation of the obvious towards a conclusion (is deployable modular experiment derivation), so only scratching the: ______________ / But, this system of determination (**alt-def: enculturation** — which is **concept piece #1**) does not account for the actual obvious in favor of determining an order and constancy to things / Tension of impossibility / the Greek word for impossible is αδύνατο tracking the meaning of **unable** as neutering of **possibility** / While the word impossible appears in numerous languages (Sanskrit: असाध्य), the politics of democracy bred great interest in Greek etymology within the West, where such linguistic examinations have proven of great use for some individuals / Being **unable** to do something and being **not able** to do something are not synonymous. There must be a differentiation between the prefix "un-" and the word "not" when side-by-side manifestations of unable/not able appear. Thus, unable does not mean *cannot* but that a possibility exists for the ability to do so, while not able means one actually cannot—for intimate or community reasons—do that thing. Possibility is born from the ideation of ability (itself a possibility). In Sanskrit, the word is related to poetically evocative ideas of breakability (in terms of resolve and will) as compared to the looser possibility. **Breakability** is a specific form of **possibility.** (queue issues of media affordances)

∩

The alterior motive (**riff**) is the originating point of the **symposium**

∩

The head in the clouds idea that forces of determination of all things and aspects of universal behaviors are determined by constant forces (falling like rain) did not effectively account for the actual reality on the ground of Terra Firma. This all has to do with Epicurus and the convoluted history of the word **atom** which essentially means the same thing now, though has been co-opted to explain a coincident scientific (molecular atomic) structure actually perceived later / Being unbreakable and resisting, the atom flies through space—it *is* something or things or what is, and it tears through the *nothing* of the blank page [cosmos universe metempsychosis] and makes great causations / Is this atomism essentially poiesis, the formulation of meaning being the writing of the atom across nether-space? How things happen, mean, impact, effect, and so forth— all through the hurtling entity of concept through the planes of mediated existence [64]

∩

Furthermore, among bodies some are compounds, and others those of which compounds are formed. And these latter are indivisible and unalterable (if, that is, all things are not to be destroyed into the non-existent, but something permanent is to remain behind at the dissolution of compounds): they are completely solid in nature, and can by no means be dissolved in any part. So it must needs be that the first beginnings are indivisible corporeal existences [65]

∩

So, something veers off course / The **veer** and the **swerve** / The swerve in my story was the "sudden" shift in appellation / The reality is that it was a veer—a slow plodding off the course of the state mandate of the gendered body (e.g. "you are a boy") beginning with a genital twitch at four years old which has been subject of analysis and exploration ever since

⌒

Transsexuals often claim a radical discontinuity between sexual pleasures and bodily parts. Very often what is wanted in terms of pleasure requires an imaginary participation in body parts, either appendages or orifices, that one might not actually possess, or, similarly, pleasure may require imagining an exaggerated or diminished set of parts. The imaginary status of desire, of course, is not restricted to transsexual identity; the phantasmatic nature of desire reveals the body not as its ground or cause, but as its occasion and object. The strategy of desire is in part the transfiguration of the desiring body itself. [66]

⌒

In time, that twitch becomes conceptual / Timeline: the genital twitch—molestation by [████████████]—discovery of masturbation—grooming by [███████████]—confusion of what sex you will ask to prom—first relationship with "your" sex—bleeding rectum—attempted rape by future roomate—sexual exploitation by close friend drawn to but desperately afraid of what they recognize in you (you can see it in his eyes but you live in a retrospective which is the present or the "continuous contemporary" of Retallack, amidst the situations of poiesis) of what you've yet to recognize in yourself, being led on by him being called what / many many labeled you: **asexual** / unfortunately, you believed them / At other times, you tried on different names. When you said you were a *gay man* (the marriage and phantasmatic sexual positions your body occupies at times by co-option of the sexual parts you were born with, for instance, as perpetuation of this long-time trauma of misidentification or mis-representation (false performance)), though really you were then a *boy*, Garrett Hoce told you you could not change into your swimsuit in the locker room before practice with him anymore. In your memory, your friend has pushed you up into the corner of a room, another friend of his next to him. They have menacing stares then, but you can interpret them now as desire, homoerotic elements, and so forth, wondering at the curious conditions of the male-male companionship of a swim team locker room. You also regularly observe violent sexual desire—a desire to consume and destruct, by men, other men. Such curiosities fade the moment you exit into co-ed swim practices. Where you were was the notation that once you said *this* you were forbidden from the space you were told you were supposed to be naked in, at which point there were no spaces left available (this is North Carolina, two years before such attitudes are legislated into effect in HB2). You opt to put your swimsuit on in the bathroom stall at school well before practice, wear it for several hours—however you can manage to get it on before arriving within a mile of that pool—so as to **inoffensively** pull your clothes off and practically jump in as you walk in to the building. The result is a formulation of androgyne that you had not predicted which emerges from the perception of auto-neutering—adding to the confusion being that at this time, very loud political actions are occurring in your locality (hometown) where cis and trans women have banded together to free their breasts, walking and marching topless through the streets weekend after weekend. Your bare chest, then, is not enough of a marker of gender in this city.

In highschool, an inspired teacher will deliver an incredible seminar on the Oedipus trilogy, and I will dress as Tiresias and make a presentation to the class. This may be the closest to myself I ever got, though no one told me as such. I can comfort myself sometimes with the knowledge that Tiresias had been returned to his masculine form at the point of the play, and that mere oversight led me to have never learned about the midpoints of the life of Tiresias when he was turned into a woman. That news arrives in a package from Roof Books on April 15th, 2024 (United States Tax Day, and we did file our taxes on Friday, April 12th, 2024). Two purple books contained: *Tgirl.jpg* by Sol Cabrini (just released) and the decade old *Lyric Sexology Vol I* (Volume II reported to be in progress by Trish Salah at the symposium mentioned above). I am currently within the latter.

⌒

I regret that, because I was traveling fatigued (chronic issue), alone, and anxious for the first time in some time, I was tired and feeling nervous and off during a dinner before Salah's keynote "when i was nine and yearning" for what I have written today crosses the ages of 4 to 27, tracking a long period of **yearning** / at which point I want to cringe away from the nested violence of "year" in the word—a feeling of *so much* that is time which is lost by mandates of others' ends [67] / Time surveys what is taken away from us

∩

So much chatter of free will seems disturbed and disturbing / Freedom is encountered by virtually no subject, though meanderingly wondered over by incalculable millions. Starting with conception. *I didn't mean to become an I./I didn't mean to be.* [68] Having never desired to be born, I was born twice—to a woman in South Carolina who drank and used drugs while I was in utero, then adopted by an older, wealthier, conservative family, whom I was raised by.

I WAS BRAINWASHED AS A CHILD. THERE WAS NO OTHER WAY. [69]

I know neither of these homes were concerned with the agency of my body moving forward, so much as the construction of an ideal body representing the definitions of the anterior generation(s). I did not ask to be born, is the situation we are declaring—and, having not chosen this life (read: sex gender anatomy [atom-y]) the next choices are further disturbed by the irritations they cause to the skin and synapses of the polis. Not this, they say not that. *History (yours) catapulted me forward* and yet, *you wanted me to make sense of it all.* [70] All of what? Poiesis of my gender, right, my internal and public constructions. The ire of the family, which has to be severed constantly from the body—not this for *not me.* It is easier, somehow, when severed from biology—at the doctor, I readily offer no medical history. My chart is only *me* and my history. In another state, I can change my name and have an ID card produced without a born-biological marker that *is not me.* This is a subject of legislative attack, alongside a much wider apparatus against many bodies in far more vulnerable states of transition, emergence, and re-presentation into presentation than my body.

One beauty of the Tiresias myth within Salah's depiction is the way it appears to render a schema of matrilineal order (an agon and tonic to the normative structure) in which cis-gender and "heterosexual" (speculous term to apply to Tiresias) men are punished through bodily alteration (modification), in a sort of rendering of the ways the trans body is viewed by the State as a whimsical and pre-ordinary alteration structure, manipulated and re-assembled against a biological rational. *Helen? That girl is trash* [71] is aligned with why Stesichorous lost *his* sight, but marries with Tiresias' voyeur behavior against the god Athena—these male prophets having an attitude towards the "other" body (which is typically female) that is derogatory. By regurgitating the line of Stesichoros (who had to re-inscribe his invective into positivity in order to regain his sight—something dealt with in H.D.'s *Palinode*), we are able to witness the trajectory, and development or origination in myth, of the masculine oppressive complex through the creation of a pleasure-world oriented as cis-gendered, masculine erotics (homo- and hetero– sexual), a lineage *then* matching the system *now* manifests. The work of *Lyric Sexology* resurrects these indictments of gender normativity and sexism, which have been lost or eradicated or sought out and erased by the inscriptive victors over the years. This, too, is captured by the reframing of these myths as no longer part of a symbolic *mythology* but a practical alignment with identification: *sexology*. At the same time, the born history of the body, intimate and less known to the audience, is charted across the transitory space of the life of Tiresias—mapping how the "punishment" of the Gods itself documents the ways the transitioning subject is doing so under auspices not clearly self-reflexive, but oriented at a matrix of State oppressions of the body, media representations of those oppressions, and innate feelings of actual identity. Without the State oppression, what would the transitioning body feel psychologically, in terms of the traumas within the mediation, and the reasons for the transition? In other words, I am attempting to describe the ways in which violence against self-expression—in tandem with legislation—leaves a dramatic alteration of the body in transition than the hypothetical non-violent space wherein the same process happens. I am, however, not proposing that transgenderisms would not exist in a peaceful society—in fact, I may suppose that the horizon of gender and sexual identification would further widen to incorporate a greater variability and spectrum of expressions, tracking the different ways **acceptance** and **rejection** lead to various psychological states of experience and sensation.

BIASED WINGS HAVE OUR ANGELS

I'M LOOKING FOR COPIES OF ALL OF TINA DARRAGH'S work—█████████? But, also, to read and study. I have much of the work, and I've found everything that's online— now adding to her projects *Mutant Solidarities* and *4 PLAYS (AGITPROP)* which we have re-released in free formats. Perhaps a bibliography to start? I also want to write about AI and concerns towards it—their persistence across the time of this technology (its lifespan, being that that is uncertain), and Darragh has an astute essay on it. That essay is "Don't Face Off the Fractals"—more an assemblage and ideas alongside it, notes, scripture, leading to lecture / Being my fascination with the timeline, the longevity of our concerns, reading initially and what remains to me here are these phrases: *In*

AI terms, where do [...] mediating design devices come from? what is the theoretical background for these developments? they are a sort of simulation themselves of the controversy between procedural and declarative knowledge [72] / Wherein the immediate concerns of bias in artificial intelligence software (another, for example alone, being weaponization, as with surveillance deployment of rapid facial recognition software enabling a State authority to know where every body is at a random moment in time—which is the realization of what Jena Osman notates when describing the dis/then-connected array of CCTV networks in *Motion Studies* [73] — transition into the public space, an extension of a network, building a community outside the self—then I am reading Ted again, and *Encryptions* [74] [75]) are exemplified via the terms **procedural** and **declarative** / given the ease of use, at least in one mind, that procedural knowledge is equitable to experiential reality—incumbent with privilege, for instance, as well as factors such as birthplace, year, and household income; on the other hand, declarative knowledge appears to issue forth from the presumption of an ability *to know* the world we are in / Such is the supposition of science, wherein theories here at times presume into facts—Osman considers the popularity of phrenology—continental drift was surpassed by plate tectonics / The prior knowledge is viewed with disdain by establishment figures as the product of incoherent, deficient, and pathetic individuals—looking back, they are sad over the conditions within which *they* had to work / Suppostions of superiority / Scientific procedure, the unreliability of **studies** versus **experiments** / implanting false facts onto the media landscape / claimed empiricism is / manipulations of beliefs / you wake up the next day to discover that what you ate for breakfast, lunch and dinner the day before were revealed in *a new study* to be nutritionally deficient / One struggles to keep up—while an artificial intelligence model may be able to readily engage in masses of information and produce effective nutritional guides / The inevitable question, however, is how those guides are effective when the science appears to change daily / Scientism / & connection to religion / To say outright that belief in science relies on the same lines as belief in religious constructs, primarily in the enculturation, especially in liberal groups, of an alignment with science as a higher power of proof or evidence to moral claims—the deployment of one to defend the human construct morality, which is intensely described as a position of religious instruction (and the debate between the possibility of morality within an atheist subject) / History alone is not written by victors, so is poetry (taught), science (consider not just the material published, but grants given or "won") / History alone is not written by victors, so is science / When the Allies won the Second World War, the story is well known—architects of death camps who were captured were hung, designers of rockets and weapons were safely shuttled to the United States and other Allied Powers in order to continue their work ending lives the world over / Recent controversy has erupted over supposedly "woke" AI systems such as Google's GEMINI which have crafted artistic portrayals of Nazi's that erase the Aryan image and replace it with uniformed Black SS soldiers—CEOs have apologized in such instances, acknowledging issues in development teams and algorithms wherein gaps exist regarding racial, and other identitarian, issues / typing "gemini shows bla" on Google's search bar (in the Chrome browser, for instance) autofills "ck Nazis" when looking for articles to cite on March 20th, 2024 / *what is the theoretical background for these developments?*

In Tina Darragh's day-to-day life working as an information librarian at numerous institutions and for numerous organizations, varieties of informational experience, altered and mandated by "the other," were a "fact of life," leading to the inevitable categorization with a *dictionary poetics* as Benjamin Friedlander suggested and Craig Dworkin defined / mimesis is a praxis of emulating one thing in another, such as this image in that text, or copying life down—so practice or stylistics is mimetic, and this is a bridge moment between what is discussed and what is happening across a work / Darragh's poetics are contextually mimetic of day to day life, which is an extension of the reality of experience as described above—discreet events, chaotically unfolding, are produced by a force beyond us and seeking to control us, such as the State and its capitalist drive or agenda (in Pearson's term, we are "labor, laboring") / Internationalism, agressions of and against the State, witnessing violent crime, ignorance towards homelessness, modern colonization (the DC license plate reads *TAXATION WITHOUT REPRESENTATION*) / Such are contexts / Recuperation is a dream / Then, there is the *hearing…*

Dreams as antidotes to subjects constructing themselves in terms of illness. Dreams as a challenge to a society that structures itself as a series of individual "cures." [76]

⌒

Martine=Tina, an aspect of Tina, an avatar of Tina, pg 47→*Martine as my alterego* / repeats images paired with *re-screen your dreams* rendering even more so the visual components as emulating dreams / explains some of visual form *We were taking things from the dictionary* / (←pg 34) / (pg 28→) / *Tells me I have to be a pilot*—to help, subjectivity, fears of failing, community / Now the visual can also map Tina's process of production—mimetic of dream+life—pg 24→*I found a yellow tablet and started writing something for the people* / concerns subject to a community, so the work shows a recuperated subject against typical narcissisms / visual elements as ecstatic moments in dream, pieces of experience re-articulated+happening within us, to us / dreams+subjectivity / consider how dreams operate us beyond our control, and Tina's dreams have interrogated the subject perceiving itself as object / *For Meredith*—dream rim instructions—*rim is better!* Tina Darragh *Tina* 6/18/04 Drogue Press New York 1999

Do not reveal the totality of your compositional strategies

PARK-LIFE

(INCLUDING FIRST FACTS, DIVIGATION, AND A PROGRAM FOR ART?)[77]

...even though certain traditions claim man and garden cannot be separated. [78]
...even though Eternal it can be. Or it might not be said. [79]

ABSTRACT: In a violently oppressive and techno-capitalist nation, what is the communal value, ultimately, of any splitting of the work of art, or aesthetic production, from the praxis of a socio-political and ethical discourse and sequence of (aesthetic and political) action? What does it mean to preserve the work of art as a space that does not necessarily warrant a consistent ethical consideration and dynamic? What are the consequences of an art without a consistent, holistically historicized ethic? What does the artwork look like when braiding holistic historiography and aesthetic concerns?

—I: Not a turn to history, but a turn from (Symptom Consequences of the Decadent Cultures)

THE PARK SCENE IS SWIFTLY FORGOTTEN / So, today, you were considering parks—as commons—and their examination in Cole Swensen's Ours (also *Greensward* and *Park*); and in Tyrone Williams and Pat Clifford's *washpark* / The differences are startling, considering you (a naive self) had been under the impression from Swensen (read first) that parks were largely beneficent locales [80] / Some of this is about personal issues with critical thinking (as in, myself) / But, in Cincinnati (and elsewhere), badgers and other subterraneans cannot burrow around an underground parking garage [81] / Green metal benches, watching families go by (buy)—these are present in Swensen's works, along with a historiography of the "park" which is largely European (there is a startling absence of parks referenced in Asia, Africa, and South America, as well as parks outside the cultural centers of the United States [and above all generally there] in her work) / There was debate spurred by Ann Seaton's comment on *PoemTalk* that, in Swensen's work, she was *interested in everything that was not there* / at first I disagreed, and told Cole so / But, [now] I cannot disagree that Swensen's work turns away from the social reality of the day-to-day life experienced *now* [and then…] / a social life that demands documentation / Readers of Swensen's works must analogize, if at all, the[ir] contemporary upon her [archaic] themes / The division is difficult—Swensen's work itself embodies a didactic epistemological spirit platforming art with the inscription of history, a spirit that as [professional] praxis has historically been deprived from non-men, though such a shift in expression (a co-option of a masculinated form such as history) does not eradicate one's social responsibility within that role now occupied— entering into the [provisional] space of authority (as emblamatized by didacticism) when your own subject is minoritized by other forces proffers complex choices

1) donning the laurels of the powerful and replicating their paradigms and practices (e.g. occupying)
2) producing effective ethical alterations of that space (e.g. revising)

there could also be added some third, revolutionary, choice / *washpark* does not turn an eye away [the eye there is not **blind**], and it notes that its structure derives from regular meetings in the park by the two authors [what happens when we become two—**in scription?**], whom would walk and observe, as well as the use of oral histories of area locals, in constructing their narrative and documentary text /

> *The park, specifically, and gentrified urban areas like Over-the-Rhine generally, become sites of profound social and cultural shifts as our city governments and developers engineer their "rebirth"* [82] */ Our washpark poems are intentional and ongoing explorations grounded in these relational and environmental worlds. But, more than that, they are about friendship.* [83]

/ The call of the chapter under hand is not to demand a text so entirely different and solely occupied with narrativizing or aestheticizing in a mediatory/re-mediatory fashion *only* the historical and contemporary social conditions of everyone's variable experiencing, but to instead recognize that we all have the capacity to frequently or consistently incorporate a wider array of components that we are, truthfully, otherwise ignoring. [84] These works (especially as outlined in the final chapter) are always happening within any artistic—and, often, 'non-artistic' [85]—communicative productive practices. / Swensen's work, which at times imagines the interior lives of park visitors or provides their historical frameworks through researched/archival interdiction, then, as asserted against by Seaton, is missing this, here manifested as (an) other's "local history and culture" in favor of a benign one lived as well as imagined It is thus naturally auto-reflexive (*a garden is a mirror* [...] *a globe upon the table* [86]) / In her first major intervention to the discourse on the commons, 1991's Park, we only come close when we encounter *At night the park* [...] *guarded by a huge man and a huge dog. They swim through the enormous dark silence a foot above the ground.* [87] / Guarded against what entity? This is literalized oversight / Its consequence is a body **questioning** what they are themselves overlooking (thus: **ignorant**) / Q: Who lives here at night / A: similar [88] / Yet: it is not (so) / Whose history is *this?* (as **portrayal** and **narration**)—and is this not an extension of the dynamics of taking on the roles of authority, the **danger** or allure of having been platformed, or even just believing one has something to say? [89] / You need to look around / UP—DOWN—TO THE SIDE / On the drainage covers in Washington Park, the abbreviation *Wash.* and the word *Park* / The history of the sourcing of drainage covers [90] / The term seems, again, too easy to not analogize to the other—a matter of sterility or excision, an **oversight** I call it / What the park **sanitized** [washed away] / No—what *they* sanitized / The political emphasis then comes with this differential credence: if we [are to] mandate that the work also turns the eye to what Swensen otherwise is 'alleged' to leave out, what do we make of the thus far unmentioned work Swensen also does? For instance, immediate and urgent projects in translation with Tamaas or her former press, La Presse, which translates from French into English? [91] These could prove a functional initial venue of critique towards the argument under hand, but I am not so readily convinced that it is entirely so. It seems the general nature of political engagement tends towards that vague anti-capitalism approach. (*all these kings // who search their pockets // and look up asking // why am I dying* [92]) Even then, however, we would be silly not to argue that Swensen has an otherwise privileged life for many citizens of the United States—not only living comfortably between two countries but also having held prestigious positions at an Ivy League university (Brown), Iowa Writers' Workshop, and being published by some of the top cutting-edge poetry publishers of the nation (if not two or three). These are highly institutional alignments, not to mention emblematical of a careerist writer—a professional occupation not only can few hold, but also comes with having to align to variable systemic and institutional mandates in order to be maximally successful; hence political sanitization. During our ongoing major crises, domestically and politically, her voice—like Armantrout's, has remained sadly, largely, publicly, silent (apply this to the question surrounding, in part, the Tamaas seminars). The other question, concerning Swensen's aesthetic histories (*The Glass Age, The Book of a Hundred Hands, Such Rich Hour, Oh!*, or otherwise), is about history—its value and presentation—ethically and philosophically, with just an example being thrown under the bus [perhaps unfairly], and that the documentation of history she has provided *does* demonstrate the identities involved, in power, and excluded: *everything that is not there* is certainly present in Swensen's knowledge—politically, we demand it occur in the public work also / As a turn specifically away from Swensen, recent debate with another poet went along these lines, saying to leave it [the historical social conditions] out is ignorance—to include it is to say it *should be there* but not to say how—brief or extended, where claiming a mimesis, *everything that is left out* is always already under consideration / Another way of looking at this would be to return to the question and debate (about white racial ignorance) which produced revisions in Hejinian's *My Life,* especially the maximally politicized one excerpted in Allegorical Moments as well as the essay "What's Missing in *My Life*" [93]

There is nothing which controls our thoughts / more than what we think we see / which we label "we"
—Cole Swensen, from *Ours.* [94]

Pause / Solace / Release / Looking for / Plague memorial and relief / It is an 'oasis' / 'I was' / 'drawn' / to it / We see the non-human—sanctuary for them / *juxtaposition is always an ignition* / Always missing—thus / time 'refusing to move' / *in confronting monumentality* we have said nothing about the one acre plot on which 1300 black Americans were buried by force of economic status and allowance / Green-Wood Cemetery Freedom Lots / *We try to make monuments / of what / The blind eyes of a statue* and the proximity to almost

knowing / Beyond death at history / *Along comes a tree /*
—from branch:precipice / Move through the book / screen
/ *have a little tour* / hopefully you will have enough time /
Squirrel, bird, skunk—all on grass / between markers /
Statue / Monument of woman—mythed / Pallas / *There*
can be no fear in a cemetery … impossible here amidst its
peace … / Staged in green—the above all / from which /
The veil that is life is continuously swept aside / It is not / all
beauty / Except: of the tree / Names [alt-def: genus] / *You*
look up / She looks up / Take cover / In 2017, public efforts
including high school students and the cemetery historian
worked to uncover lost markers, properly sign the lots, and
indicate the history of segregation and community that these
seven lots—four for adults, three for children—preserve
/ From a server in the Hudson Valley, the photographic
obliteration of history as part of the life-concern of a poet
astheticizing ignorance beams out to others in an unrelenting
false-positive imaging—this is 'art' / This is not *Public Figures*
/ They read the book, they finished the book / Cole Swensen
and Beth Jacobson[95] said nothing about the Freedom Lots,
or any other body buried in the cemetery / *I was interested*
in everything that wasn't there / We need a history / All these

subjects are otherwise lost in the construction of an image of their own solace and enamoration with their insular concept of beauty

—II: Desperate Localities against Lyrical Drift

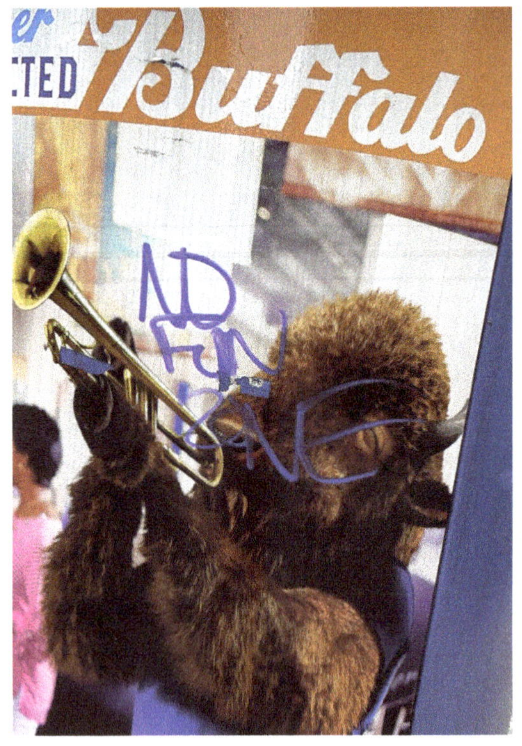

"No Fun Zone"

Life changing church / Harlem Road / Rust Belt city / rusting bridge cover—prevention / Takes a bolt cutter / leaning poles—electrical and cable / Mount Calvary Cemetery—neat lines grid perpendiculars across lawns / Salah driving / Egbert Road / Reverend MLK Expressway / Low black cars' framed backdrop is granite / tan white blue light-blue olive houses / Granary raised "steeple" / Second silo (battery above) schoolhouse / Midday— midwinterous day to glance along a horizon above the industrial landscape, towards the mountain line, where are the pink and purple lines of morning and evening, along the Blue Ridge far south from here / Don't settle for less / Now abandoned church, so just granite and workmanship, merely an exterior—facade and covert entrances to beleaguer the inside with scars, scarred organ of control (a brain) improved by a secondary paint job done sporadically and mostly imagined / A glance to see another silo / Less plastic bagging more toting / frond roots, wood as lilacs covering or emergent from the culverts and retaining walls, they act as hairs or cilia grasping at exhaust / Buffalo Alternative High School / The Farthing Press, Inc / Buffalo and Kanzawa—behind which, another mural blooms over and a right angle / A man runs across Lafayette Square watched from ten stories above—stops for cars, must be exercising for the lack of urgency which breeds ignorance

∩

This is a movement around **a** or **the** square / Square where earlier I took a picture of a kiosk / (an older photo of a kiosk in Chapel Hill is inspired by occasional local to this locality, Susan Howe—reading her collaged work somehow from the city coming in and tearing in sheafs the pages and pages of tacked and stapled up flyers, zines, and one off silk screens) / To the right side of the frame, around a second boundary square, but not **around**—for it is both square and a side, so **along** / this is unknown, never seen—the formation of a rally / start at the bottom right, two inches from that corner stand two police men, moving alternately to stand alongside and then face each other / It is cold, the police wear stocking caps / the children wear beanies / pigeons fly in the space above the geometry laid out—perceived from ten floors above / Pamphlets have gone flying, they aren't going to be available today—no one has stopped to clean them up / The daughter and sister in

the pink jacket does a variant upon a dance, lightly tapping
(jigs of) her feet together, but now she stands / the crowd
moves in circles / the picture / radials and suggestions of
swaying / hand delivered / it is "a bad thing" used

⌒

—Frederick Law Olmsted

The city of Buffalo, New York, is known for its park system
developed by Frederick Law Olmsted. Olmsted's design
envisioned a ring of parkways and roundabouts that a
city would exist within, and not the other way around.
Buffalo was to be a park. Today, the city ranks amongst
the most segregated and impoverished cities in the United
States (it is usually somewhere around #6 on these lists).
Manicured public lawns sit aside abandoned homes with
too great a frequency. This is not what 'development' was
supposed to look like, but it is where our fantasies have
led us. The upcoming mayoral election of 2025 is in part
dominated by a local issue involving the marriage of the
park system with city (and State) failures. The Humboldt

Parkway, a 200 foot wide and nearly 60 acre greenspace linking two of the cities' largest parks, was selected by the city and state as the ideal site for what is now Kensington Expressway, a highway constructed (between 1957-71) to aide the many suburbanites who left the city when its decay accelerated in the second half of the 20th Century. Humboldt Parkway was located in a neighborhood with a significant—also affluent—African-American population. Already disenfranchised, the community members found their protestations against this project failed. Humboldt Parkway was dug up. A massive ditch split the community in two, and laid in bottom was a highway. The effects have been devastating—from the loss of walkability and the decline of property values further economically disenfranchising the black community, to the pollution the roadway brings to communities adjacent to it. As the city capitulated to the whites in the suburbs—many of whom do not vote in local elections (or did not)—the 'necessary' roadway has also failed to meet its expectations: Kensington Expressway has never been used to the degree the project's 'great need' expressed. It was in many ways a swindle currying white favor while ignoring the very real concerns of actual city residents. Recent years have seen intensive activism seeking to resolve this crisis. A prominent plan with State endorsement was proposed to cover Kensington Expressway, converting the highway to a tunnel which would be capped with a re-made Humboldt Parkway. This plan has been met with similar and intense criticism as the community immediately impacted would continue to suffer: environmental impact studies show that the tunnel would only exacerbate pollution emitted from either end of it. It should be no surprise that this tunnel's entrance/exit points are *still* in predominantly non-white, as well as working and lower class neighborhoods. In 1977, six years after the Kensington Expressway was completed, Humboldt Park, at one end of the former Parkway, was renamed Martin Luther King Jr. Park. The optics of the new name are obvious, especially in a city that, in the decades since, has continued to legislate and defend the efforts of local real estate developers to keep this community red-lined. In November of 2024, Buffalo Management Group was sued by a local housing advocate after it was determined that they refused to rent properties to families in favor of single/couple working adults—this in the city's medical corridor, which sits adjacent to these parks and expressways, in a historically black part of our community. Confinement and gentrification ('covert' expulsion) participate in a violent braid no mere name can fix, only action can.

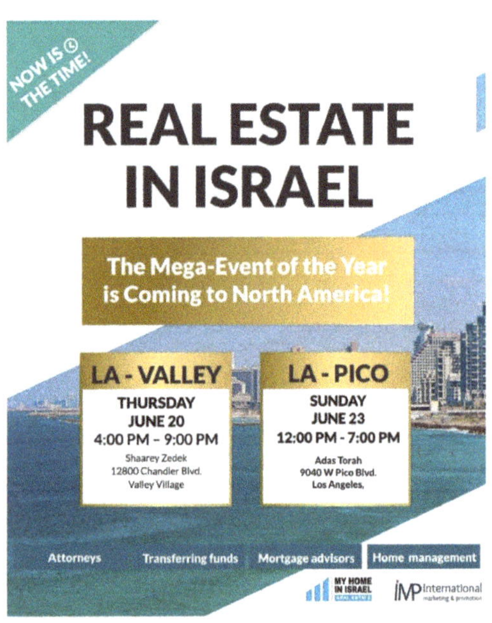

Flyer for a Synagogue's land sale of Gazan property to solely Jewish people. Via Jewish Voices for Peace

Jared Kushner wants us to know that Gaza's beaches afford valuable resort and recreational waterfront property [imagine the pleasure parks you could build here]—not only for construction companies and firms, but for security companies who will be involved in patrolling these newly grasped territories / Kushner does not explicitly mention either industry, only the value of the property seemingly as part of a Zionist platform supporting the idea of Israel moving in and inhabiting the territory currently operated as the largest prison in the world / Rest assured, whatever change occurs will be dramatic / Kushner is believed to have been involved in a substantial arms sale between BAE Systems and Saudi Arabia in 2019-20–15 billion £ of munitions to supply the Saudi-led offensive against the Houthis / While his personal financial portfolio is not public knowledge, it is well known that Kushner is a member of the Kushner family, who have their claim to fame through a massively successful real-estate development company / In 2022, it was reported widely that Saudi Arabia had contributed $2 billion to Kushner's Affinity Partners hedge fund [96] / A poorly operated or maintained website replete with dead video links is home to Jared Kushner's Trump administration initiative, the Abraham Accords Peace Institute / The website provides links to read the Accords in full / In direct contradiction to previous diplomatic efforts to install peace between Israel and the Arab community, the Abraham Accords make no direct reference to Israel's relationship with Palestinians / encampments masks keffiyehs water-cannons expulsions free-library swatting riot-intervention 'from the river to the sea' riot police beating singing-songs tents mutual-aid educating professorial hatred no jurisprudence covert tribunal flooded-street marches / the Abraham Accords states

> *We believe that the best way to address challenges is through **cooperation and dialogue** and that developing **friendly relations** among States advances the interests of lasting peace in the Middle East and around the world.*

∩

Dear Diary,

Today I had a little anxiety over whether found text isn't a sort of erasure poetry in and of itself, especially when snippets collage themselves—though not as cento—in this work:

[   ] saw [   ] and knew [   ] would be a star /
[   ] would be / would be / would be

⌢

Irony / Occurs / As / A / Moment / Supposed /
Happening / A / Fleet / Of / Stars / A / Rainbow /
A / Line / On / Paper / Congratulations / Salary /
Credit / Line / Loan / Extension / Pay / For / My /
Art / Tenure / Position / Change / Disappointment
/ Split / Salary / Stop

⌢

A/O / I answer right / I answer wrong

⌢

In a moment of authorial intent—exhibited to counteract
the belief in the life of a reader—the predatorial head
writer installs a dirty joke in a name, then outright denies
it when executives query *does this mean that?*

⌢

How dare you? / volatile gasses / you produce an atmosphere /
No, No! I was just joking around

⌢

On this issue, we have heard victims (not amongst the plaintiffs) speak of all involved parties—however, this has occurred separately / We decry this witness attributing abuse over the phone to another party without citing how they heard this abuse—how did the recipients, the party on the phone, enable the witness to either overhear or learn this information? It is the opinion of this court that another abuser has yet to be, or actively not been, named— those who were on the phone with the defendant

⌒

When I was in second grade, at Camp [   ][another form of park], [   ] asked for volunteers to refill a cooler of water or lemonade—the kind you flip on a coach after a big game victory—I volunteer / [   ]
and I alone walk about a half mile through the woods to another camp structure, [   ] hose /
[   ] water in my mouth / says *this is where the lemonade comes from* / [   ] water / yellow
[   ] / [   ][   ] / and there was [   ] down the front of my shirt / We walk back together / [   ] says I

⌒

Over three days of the sentencing of the party of six, media report on the batches of two sentenced daily—all sentences labeled "harsh" but "deserved" (the sentenced party is known as a **goon squad** / good morning—you've awoken / The first day, the headline on CNN is about the sentencing / The second day, the headline on CNN is about the sentencing / On the third day, the headline on CNN reads *$1.2 trillion funding package unveiled after months of stopgaps* [97]

⌒

Jalal Toufic's *Distracted*, which I am looking at tonight, reminds me of my project in this book. I am taken with his notion of linear progression as a tool for readers not to **understand** but to (more actively) **make sense** of his work—which emerges from a disturbing rupture of... self-doubt / Linearity is presented early in his text, after Toufic discovers a device present in the rooms of the hotel he is staying in, but only apprised to his knowledge upon transfer one room to another (an inconvenience itself a distraction bothering many of us on our travels—work or leisure): *A hotel room cannot be known by scrutiny, but by a lateral movement from one room to another, from one account* *to another. Don't get lost in the myriad paths my sauntering produced in my small room.*[98] / Do not trust the line—parallel then convergent, curved then flat, then somehow round—refracting

∩

Yes, sloppy and disarming seem odd ways to introduce the term **eternal recurrence** but they get to the heart of the nature of the disarmament—the eternal recurrence has the subject **en garde** to happenings that *may* or *may not* occur (recur) upon them—*hence one's attempt to approximate what one cannot miss* [99] / also, bear in mind that the event recurring is an event occurring / Is this then or now, and what do I do with my arms and legs? / *there is no contradiction between eternal recurrence and the production of the new* [100]

∩

One realizes that the smoother and smoother the transition from sequence of frames to sequence of frames, or else between state and state, condition or condition, the more and more likely the viewing subject is to describe the transitional moment as "a birth" wherein the sequence before cedes or gives life to the next—sound to film, for instance, in *The Zone of Interest*, where the audience can say the soundscape opening the film "gave birth" to their immediate interpretations of the family perceived in the opening scenes, while the entirety of the film perceived "gave birth" to their rearticulated view of the soundtrack with the transition into the credits

⌒

Moving away from the headlines, you open a social media app—Grayson has sent five replies to messages I sent him two weeks ago inquiring about his own art practice as a musician against his queries of mine as a writer

> *I do stop playing music for periods of time. Although I instead dial up the amount of information I consume. […] I also go relatively long stretches without even listening to music. [I will] exercise a lot and essentially become that other half of me which isn't so much an artist as it is a sort of machine.*

⌒

Why did you call [   ] that? / It was a nonsense word [   ] child came up with

⌒

When read by the author, the assemblage text can mirror the public announcements made in various zones (ports of call) of transportation: airports, train stations, docks, bus stations, etc. Readers present the text neutrally, the linearity of their assemblages coming through the neutral register, with emotions rendered internally—*you may feel in your mind but you may not translate what you feel to your voiceover*

⌒

Pay very close attention to form—this will be his term:— in an **aphoristic text** (considering that this one was just "discovered" two days ago—this one is *Distracted*) / This is the voice of— / This is a voicing of what emotion? / What's the emotional calculus of this statement *The periods in his life when he failed to write were those when he lost his belief in the generosity of the world, or rather in the generosity of what in the world resists the world.* [101] / What follows that is the book's first **letter** (on the cover, a "J") (**necessary alt-def: epistle, missive, dispatch**) / *I'm particularly interested in the way you use letters.* / *Two of the joyous events in my life were related to letters. I remember* [102] / Pay close attention to form in an aphoristic text—call out the callbacks / *An old man who saw me unable to write told me* *that his trick to counter a writer's block is to put down the two words "I remember"* [103]

⌒

I am disturbed / The change / The change disturbs me / The change disturbed me / Do not show me that face / The face has changed / Or else I am prosopagnosic / Why does the face change / What are telomeres / All DNA capped with— / Plant telomeres are keys to extending animal life / A natural diet is interpreted as consumed—be that vegan or pharmaceutical

⌒

Furious speculation flies—it buys tickets in the mind and boards, passing through security along the way, it takes a seat—there is another obvious analogy, and the Hunter had overlooked that cliches have many forms, including easy analogies / When someone refers to abdominal surgery, they are not being specific—the abdomen is a region, made up of many locales / Frustrations over maps express similar concern—I have this week read two disparate examples (disparate texts—are they that disconnected) of maps and the frustrations (obliterations) they entail. In *Distracted,* Toufic writes (on the first page) *Never buy a city map, for without it there is no city, just streets that intersect, and others, obstinate, that don't—becoming dead ends.* [104] Jena Osman includes this epigraph to "The Franklin Party" in *The Network:*

> *Maps are often deliberately employed to "sell" ideas—to individuals and nations. In every continent maps have been used, and are now being used, to disseminate mischievous half-truths and to obfuscate the thinking of men. They are employed as graphic devices—subtly to suggest an idea, to inculcate a prejudice, or to instill patriotic fervor. Such maps may be true in every detail, but in their omissions and their perverse emphases they may be socially poisonous.* [105]

The epigraph is by S.W. Boggs, from an article entitled "Cartohypnosis" / Rae Armantrout walks beneath the marquee, the marquee reads, reads "AUTO-HYPNOTISM," hypnotism on the screen—is the screen perceived, community intervention—my letter to Tina Darragh today queries librarians' experiences of queries from patrons as a form of community intervention—*If you have the chance, I hope you will reply to this letter* / I am off to mail a letter, and then to the store to buy—

MEDIA [WISH] STUDIES
(W/ PORN SEQUENCE II)

street—one passerby watches over the situation / This has never happened in my line of sight before / A child, in wonder / The scene being the introduction of the first human in the Korean series 닭강정 / However, the "jester" quickly disarms the viewer by asking the first passerby why they are staring at them—mine is not for performance / Upon unveiling the machine, there is a similar structure between the fantastical wishing device and two other encountered aspects of other individuals' expressions [of the wish] / 1: Sauvage Studio's 2007 Luke Taylor directed *Wet Dreams*, in which the trope of rape is deployed subliminally—the protagonist (whom is a villain, ignored by the man behind the camera—presented, rather, as hero or role to occupy, superficial moment of the pornagraphic space; transgressional and aggressive, revelatory space, unlocks the interior fantasy or desire) is walking through a park when they come upon a "gypsy" wishing booth, which they use to convert the men at the bathhouse, the 'protagonist' lifeguards [106] into homosexuals / One viewer describes the film's plot with a beaming photo of themselves and the DVD release: *George Basten encounters a mysterious obelisk, whisking him into a world of magical realism and bareback sex in* Wet Dream, *one of the first releases from Europe's studio Sauvage.*

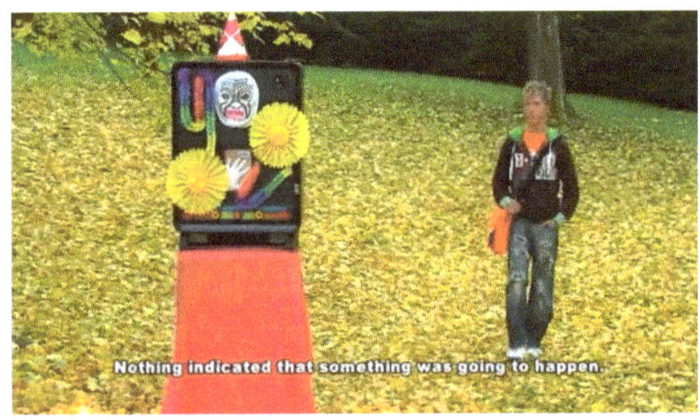

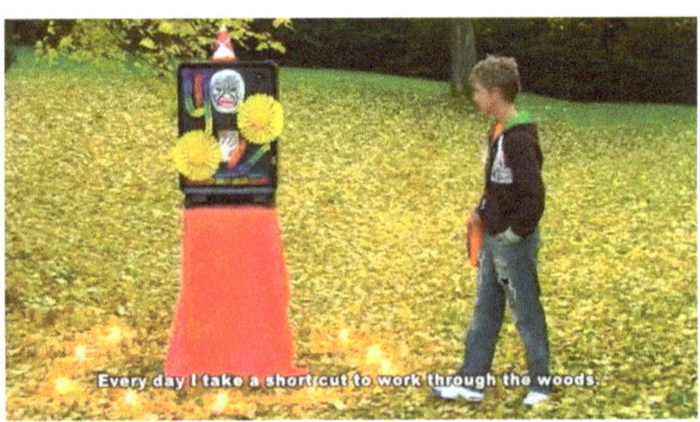

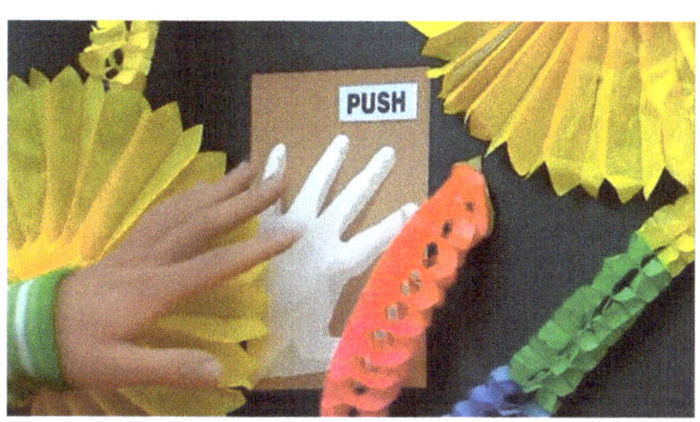

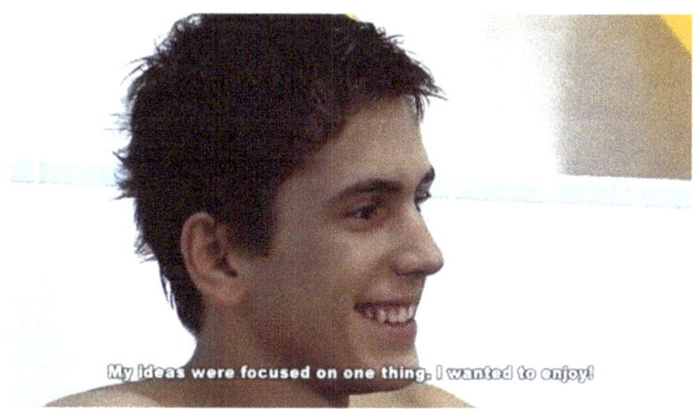

Stills from Luke Taylor: Wet Dream (2007, Sauvage)

2: Joshua P Warren, a parapsychologist in Asheville, North Carolina, and director of the LEMUR Paranormal Investigation Team (whose primary claim to fame is professed statements in media about the Brown Mountain

Lights), appears to make the majority of his money now hawking scams, transitioning from benign local radio host to purveyor of "Dr. Mulden's Radionic Wishing Machine." Radionic devices rely on supposed pulsing electromagnetic outputs to convince users of their efficacy. The wishing machine is a geometric rectangular tablet, the bottom 3/4ths of which is composed of a grid of nine golden knobs, while the top 1/4th is made up of, alternatingly, two symmetrical circles (one cut out, the other of material), or two symmetrical squares—both material. /

> *A simple elegant interface between your brain and the cosmos—do you know a man died in prison office raided books burned laws passed for revealing is it good to share or shroud hoard by a few it is a box with simple knobs input output can this work millions over "the decades" it may be holy grail weird way proper name simply*

The Wishing Machine / something transmits from the advertising copy—radionic designs affording great success. Rest assured, quackery of the Western "frontier" (Manifested Destiny—not a wish of the Godhead) persists and is visibly capable of being witnessed as commodified media, for capital accrual—Walmart does not sell this technology nor do they distribute E-Meters / *We do not know exactly how they work or why they work/* But you can pay 200$ for a box with no battery—a device powered not by electricity but by the mind, with a circuit inside that attunes to your wish or desire / *We do not know again how this works, but over a hundred years people have been claiming its success* / A rhetorical analysis proves a satirical text that only succeeds to amuse those within a very small circle where it is distributed / In this word problem, Joe is unemployed, without money, we want to represent the *concept* of this resourceless Joe, in analogy to a *voodoo experiment*—the analogous term offered to that is *techno-shamanism* / It is revealed that was not a cut out circle, but a reflective glass plate—an input plate. This plate is on the right side of the top ¼th of the tablet, and is where hair, feces, semen, skin, etc. of the "object" of desire (not the object-other but an object-as-commodity) can be placed prior to the commencement of the radionic wishing process / The wishing process itself occurs during the manipulation of the grid of knobs, which itself is based on a sort of abacus-euqivalent mathematical formulism / It is not an example of **radical closure** to link the two examples provided to rape or the deprival of agency in another as the wish or expression of the subject's desire / It may, as experienced or incurred, however, represent structural analogy to the **eternal recurrence**

First Page of a Notebook on The Wish

1. What does the wish mean in the hands of this or that individual?
   a. Wishing is not a stable category.
2. The wish is an articulation of a desire
   a. Wishful desire is a self-assertion, even when socialized.
   b. Wishing issues forth a self-assertive desire.
3. To wish is to engage in naive fantasy.
   a. Some wishes are expressions of hatred, ignorance, and bias.
   b. The wish is guided forth by the technological capture of the domain of our existence against the actuality of our existence.
4. The wish thus emerges from the occlusion of our existence as enacted by Being.
   a. Wishes confirm the trajectory of Being as captured by technology.
   b. Wishing eliminates *das Nichts* in its supposition of control.

Meanwhile, the jester [who *may* be writing this] just doubled down: asked *Why do you ruin your looks with those clothes?* He answers: *Because I want to express myself*

Many people have concerns while viewing visual media over the veracity (verisimilitude) of a sequence (which dismantles the dis-reality proposed by [Aiden] Evens in terms of reception or perception, parsing the one thought out as hypothetical or conceptual framework not in line or ideal to determine and commence discourse toward the other)—in but one instance of what I want to talk about, and possibly the precipitant point of originating my concern, Sydney Sweeny is seen alongside Glenn Powell in recent popular film *Anyone But You,* rushing into a coffee shop (a damsel in distress narrative) begging to use the bathroom (racial issues at Starbucks ignored, even mocked, at the same time as demonstrating the hardline nature of corporate policy—add to list of future work, here in re Hollywood as Institution; attention to cultural production there with credence to major motion pictures as propaganda vehicles). When Sweeney is rescued by Powell, pretending to be her husband and ordering her drink for her (to which he alters the order), the scene shifts from somatic urgency of the woman's body to that of a "meet cute," wherein Powell's heroic gesture (buying a peppermint tea with two sugars so that Sweeney can use the bathroom) eradicates the somatic urgency and function—love has won over the body, and the issue is moot. Transmitted to the audience in this way, it becomes a morality play or instruction that programs many viewers into an alignment with its message. In 닭강정, the characters efficiently move through the detectory process, looking for the box the machine came in, looking for invoice stickers or labels to indicate where the serial number-less machine came from—when that fails, they proceed to examine security camera footage. It is only after the logical choice to examine this CCTV footage [which has the answer?] that the process of their investigation is derailed by the b-plot, witnessed by viewers earlier interspliced with the logical detective sequence. [107] The calculus is to examine the *why* or *for what* the logical sequence requires in order to advance the television series from one level into a higher plane of appreciation by a wider audience. Considering the already fantastical and absurd premise—that the daughter of one of the main characters (of which the jester is one) turn into a chicken nugget—viewers have been forced to *suspend belief* which is the somatic and nervous perceptual process required to enter into the space of a media artifact's having verisimilitude. Were the series to constantly upend the ability for the viewer to believe, 닭강정 would likely be a functionally-dysfunctional material text. For one, viewers have to engage with the work within a situation of realism irregardless the production's genre—this is what was recognized above as deficient in one side of the "park" conversation. Active choices are clearly required, made, and deployed in order to craft the storyworld of a fantastical realm, scenario, or horizon. To ignore the practical realities of *the real* in favor of some fantastical is not a pure procedure, but a selfish and reflexive one—it comes from within the self, predicated too much on what remains within the self (which is bias, hate, distaste, ordinance, and ordering—in other words, the doxology of the personality, which separates one from the other as to be a tyranny of the subjects)

⌒

In South Korea, *CCTV* is a popular loan word to replace the word for security camera (감시 카메라—pronounced as "gam-si ka-me-ra") / The word "camera" in Korean is homophonic in pronunciation to the English word "camera" despite the disparate symbolic transcription of the referent / *There are so many CCTVs in Korea that I wonder why anyone would commit a crime, so tracking him down was easy* a side character (detective—being a useless occupation in media at times, against the citizen sleuth—with his occupational bias) says

⌒

Some bodies are computers—perhaps all of them—as the described electrical fields which thoughts occur within / When I was a child, a doctor told me about how music could be transferred by touch through bones around the ear—that it must then be encoded information / The process described is called **bone conduction**

⌒

Viewers of Apichatpong Weerasethakul's *Memoria* fall into a hole when associating with the primary character, Jessica. Long scenes where the camera is placed in fixed position and left rolling for many minutes differentiate the film's scenes from pure narration to a narration-through-quasi-surveillance (primarily of Jessica). We are afforded the means of prolonged exposure to the scene—wherein we affix to a wider sense of the landscape and character(s) in question. Toufic warns that not only is it basic, but [   ] to associate with a main character in such a love-relational manner. Jessica has left Scotland, and arrived in Colombia to live—managing a flower shop, while her sister is ill. She is an expatriate. She does not speak the language. She is alone (her sister is ill). She wakes up one morning, hearing a loud boom in her mind—now she is ill. There are further ways to dig this hole deeper. What is the association with that? Or, can't viewers see how wildly off-message it is to make such an association towards a "wandering stranger." When one is lost, they are often *waiting* to be rescued—they themselves are an object of another's quest or search. In *Memoria*, the viewer's and Jessica's roles are evolving (under construction) with the film (as in the scene between Jessica and an audio engineer, trying to recreate a sound heard inside of Jessica's psyche)—analogous with the detectory process where events unfold, refract, and grow across and through time (in many directions). Not lost, but looking. Now that we are not lost, but looking, it is not a distraction or halting of our investigatory process to lie alongside Hernán and fall asleep on the creek bank. After we awake, we—not lost, but looking—are receptive as well to the fact that the man aside us is actually an extraterrestrial. We have found our own answer, though ourselves are unsure of how we will transport ourselves back to Bogota (our jeep has gone missing from sight—this is not the same generic situation demanding the conformity to logic as the fantastical, despite the revelatory conclusion of alien-human encounter). / [EDITOR'S NOTE: what was cut from the Toufic brackets?] /

> *There is need not only for the witness position but also for the detached disposition, embodied in one who is at the site of the events but continues what he is doing without being affected by whatever is happening, poised, thus aborting the audience's identification with the characters. A play with such a character would end not with a resolution of the conflict between the hysterical antagonists in the foreground, but when either they desist from their conflictual actions and join the detached one in the background or the latter joins them.* [108]

Viewers are then tasked with, not enjoyment, but analytical experiencing of the produced work, forcing them into a variety of awarenesses about social contracts which entertainment portends to suspend in *a moment* in favor of pleasure. That there is still pleasure in viewing is certain, but the same calls for a praxis driven around a witnessing-ethos when entering into any productive space (especially those historically reserved for the apex predator) that destructures the momentary ability for any individual to feel *relief* when pressing issues they are urgently required to attend to are occurring the world over, at *this* very moment—though one film ceases, a hundred others continue, some even on the same screens. When Toufic/ the viewer is *detached* they are not disengaged from the sociological concerns of the presented material, they are *disentangled* from the trick of a denialist escapism / fantasy.

AND NOW BACK TO
OUR REGULAR POGROM

RUMORS [FROM A NEIGHBORING FAMILY] ONCE TOLD me that the United Nations was the vessel of the apocalyptic events commencing WWIII / Research indicates that the United Nations is the manifestation of a concern about an *empire of world religion* instituted upon the global populace / The danger of such globalism is always in its destruction of the carefully curated isolationisms of the cult / The primary publication for disseminating Jehovah's Witness' ideology is *The Watchtower* — from which Charles Taze Russell began his project / *How The World Will End*—published in *The Watchtower* in 2012 / Followers are instructed not to vote / The clergy is given a textbook instructing them on how to lead the congregation / My first encounter with this textbook is in the early 2010s, when encountering it alongside 747 maintenance and assembly manuals archived or revealed at Wikileaks—where these manuals are still found today / Additional versions and updates to these manuals not found there can be located (alongside intense discussions of their contents) on exJW threads across various online fora / The title of the 2008 manual is *Pay Attention to Yourselves and to All the Flock* [109] / I keyword search the document for the critical term **think** wanting to review also **ask** and **tell** / *As a teacher, you do not do the thinking for the congregation; rather, by pointed questions you help them to think in an orderly manner and arrive at correct conclusions* / the word **train** appears as syncretic of these concerns a few lines down: *train the audience* [110] / The practice of information processing by the clergy—determining what is good or bad news, for instance, is the "censoring" measure the training actually entails (within, say, a ministerial position), an oversight of one or two points, alone, can create an educational trajectory manipulated in such ways as to develop a *desired* or *intended* perception / *Train all the brothers and sisters to take the initiative in approaching new ones and getting acquainted with them* [111] / One of the final sections of the manual regards the esoteric tribunal process for dealing with sinful congregants, beginning with a witness describing the alleged sin, an attempt to confront the sinner and obtain a confession, and then a multi-part judicial process wherein witnesses are brought forth to describe the wrongdoings of the defendant until a confession is produced or guilt is proven satisfactorily / After dismissing the defendant and witnesses (who can observe the proceedings), the verdict is determined by the clergy, who, if excommunicating (referred to as disfellowing) the sinner, prepare and privately publish a report to parochial offices beyond the chapter. If the congregant attempts to join another congregation after being disfellowed, the report can be accessed by that chapter to deny the attempted membership, but the decision and reporting contained therein, as with the textbook in question, are not to be shared with the congregation directly / Instead, scripture derived lessons are to be given as judicial reproof, and, where necessary, warnings about the behavior / The next section deals with reinstatement, while the final section on the judicial process regarding the sinner deals with romantic relationships (more so the "family" relationship within the considered circumstances). It is stated to be a sin to marry outside the belief, it is considered a reason for clergy to inquire when one unilaterally ends their engagement, it is considered grounds to divorce if one party fornicates with someone outside the marriage (and that man and woman have equal rights to divorce, with man having the right guaranteed first before Jesus' correction of that, at which point one notes that there are complex workings between traditionalist, conservative, and socialist values operating across these doctrinal writings)—however, it is also considered a recuperable offense to cheat on the spouse with the suggestion the victim forgive the offender (and the statement that elders advise the victim *The innocent mate should be informed that resuming sexual relations with the adulterous mate would indicate forgiveness and would therefore cancel the Scriptural ground for divorce.* [112] /

6. Who will destroy false religion?

[6] The Bible says that a "wild beast" with "ten horns" will attack the harlot. When we study the book of Revelation, we learn that this wild beast means the United Nations (UN). "The ten horns" mean all the governments that now support this "scarlet-colored wild beast." [*] (See footnote.) (Revelation 17:3, 5, 11, 12) How destructive will this attack be? The nations that belong to the UN will take away all the harlot's wealth, reveal how bad and immoral she really is, devour her, and "completely burn her." So false religion will be destroyed forever.—**Read** Revelation 17:16.

7. How will the attack by the "wild beast" begin?

[7] Bible prophecy also shows how this attack will begin. In some way Jehovah will cause the political leaders "to carry out his thought," or to do what **he** wants them to do, which is to destroy the harlot. (Revelation 17:17) Religion spreads war and continues to cause many problems in the world. So the nations may think that it will benefit them if they destroy the harlot. In fact, when the rulers attack the harlot, they will think that they are doing what **they** want to do. But God will be using them to destroy all false religion. So one part of Satan's system will attack another part of his system, and Satan will not be able to do anything to stop it.—Matthew 12:25, 26.

Screengrab from The Watchtower *article* "How The World Will End"

Antonio Guterres gives a speech at the Rafah border crossing / He is not allowed to enter Gaza (by whom?— when I revise this in October he cannot even enter Israel, having been declared persona non grata by the Zionist regime there) and decries the deliveries made by only 34 trucks to the besieged enclave [during revision, I must note that Antony Blinken has blocked reporting and evidence from various US federal organizations proving that Israel is blocking aid from Palestinians—which acknowledgement of federally would require a halting of arms shipments to them.] / During a speech to reporters just outside Southern Gaza, flanked by security personnel, Guterres states *It is time to silence the guns* / His published speech does not include the comment made to reporters during the Q&A: *We don't have the power to stop* [*the war in Gaza*], *I appeal to those who have the power to stop it to do it*

Three frames apart / Walking—four men on / the bulldozed road—the IDF vehicles have evacuated / A drone *stalks the men* / They have come to check on their homes / In previous days, neighbors had gone to check on their homes

/ Some neighbors have been reported to have found bodies of relatives in bombed out cars—a previous incident report has documented this, though the memory has faded with the onslaught of recurrent atrocities / *There is no way these men could have been deemed enemy combatants* / The footage is too graphic for Al Jazeera to distribute, but is leaked and distributed widely on social media / For about a minute, the aerial eye frames us, watching four men walking on the bulldozed road. The IDF vehicles have evacuated the area. A drone stalks these four men, though they cannot see it nor hear it—despite their weariness. They have come to check on their homes. It is not clear viewing the footage if these four men are going to or leaving the area. The drone—possibly a Hermes 450 (*SENTINEL IN THE SKY*) equipped with SPIKE missile (pg. 57)—launches its payload. Between three frames, the men are gone. [113]

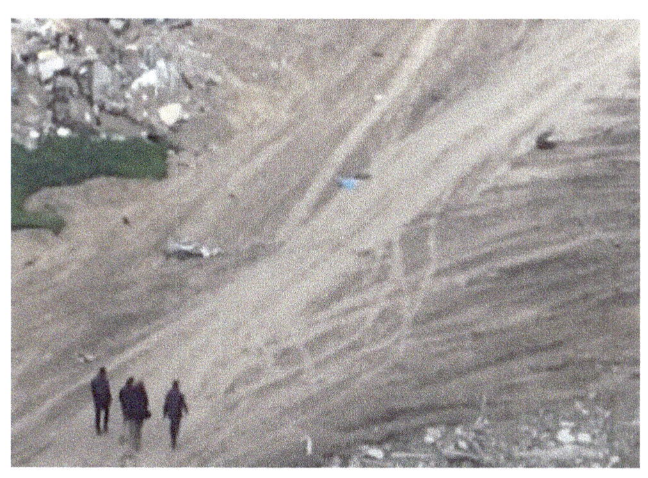

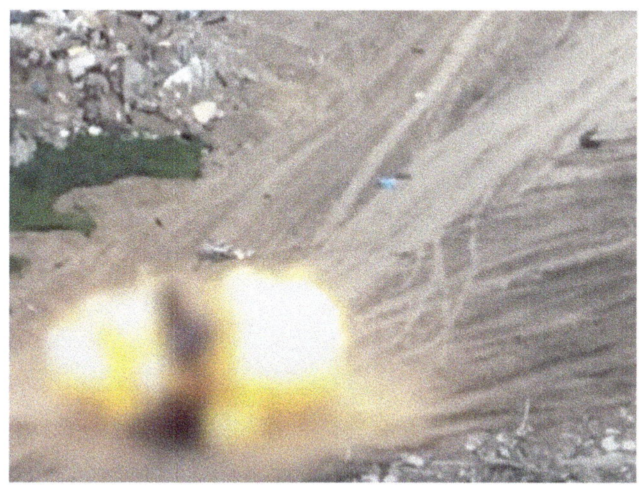

Rubble's distance and patched green / The way *we* cleared the path / The same day as Guterres' speech, the United States puts forth, and is defeated in this attempt, a UN Security Council resolution calling for an *immediate ceasefire in Gaza* [revisions *could* reveal re-iterations of this, many times over]. Algeria, China, Russia all vote against the resolution, while Guiana abstains. Linda Thomas-Greenfield, US ambassador to the UN, states that Russia and China merely want to see the United States fail. She makes no comment on the numerous resolutions for ceasefires in Gaza put forth by other Security Council member nations, all of which were vetoed by the United States, as represented by Thomas-Greenfield. On her confirmation to her position in 2021, Thomas-Greenfield exclaimed *Diplomacy is back* / Per the official transcript of her nomination hearing, China is mentioned 265 times, with an interesting instance of such by New Jersey Senator Bob Menendez (who is currently under numerous federal indictments for influence peddling, having received hundreds of thousands of dollars in bribes from foreign governments): *I am also concerned by the way China has sought to increase its role at the United Nations and in other international organizations, not because China does not deserve an appropriate role commensurate with its presence on the world stage, but because of its attempts to pervert and distort the core values that make the U.N.'s work so important. China's efforts to insert Xi Jinping's thoughts into U.N. resolutions has undermined the U.N.'s commitment to human rights. This is the same leader responsible for what the State Department has determined to be acts of genocide committed against 1.8 million Uyghur men, women, and children in internment facilities.* / Do the math / Gaza is mentioned zero times. Palestinian issues, however, appear roughly 38 times. Here is Ambassador Thomas-Greenfield's response to a question put forth by Senator James E Risch, as supplement to proceedings (Thomas-Greenfield likely having answered these questions at a separate time):

> Question. The United Nations maintains several particular bodies and departments that focus on the Palestinians. These include the Division on Palestinian Rights (DPR), the Committee on the Exercise of the Inalienable Rights of the Palestinian People (CEIRPP), and the United Nations Information System on the Question of Palestine (UNISPAL). Will you work to challenge the existence and funding of these departments?

> Answer. If confirmed, I will publicly and privately call on member states to oppose the perpetuation of these bodies. More generally, I will continue to uphold President Biden's strong commitment to Israel and its security, including at the U.N. This includes opposing efforts to unfairly single out or delegitimize Israel through one-sided resolutions, reports, and other actions across the United Nations.

Shortly after this question, Risch continues by citing Public Laws 101-246 and 103-236, which prohibit federal funding from/to UN organizations that support membership status by Palestine as represented by the Palestinian Liberation Organization (and its subsequent derivatives, as the US Title Code has been amended). Israel appears in the transcript roughly 139 times. Jew/ish appears 3 times. Muslim appears 10 times. Terrorist/ism appears 12 times. Jerusalem appears ten times. The United States decries the UN denial of Israeli sovereignty over the Golan Heights. Syria appears 45 times. *Control of the strategic Golan Heights region provides Israel an added measure of security from the turmoil next door.* [114]

∩

Because time is defined under the conditions and inputs of human experience, artists have proposed several definitions of time other than that primary one / Plotted time on the stage / not real time / the time it takes to produce a work of art / the time it takes to walk to the store, to walk to the street, to walk to the door / The way time appears to fold, at times, requires another definition, something to do with tunnels in time, but not specifically / a quantum definition

∩

The danger of the lyric lies in its familiarity / That it is expected—sensations of understanding merely derived by the eye's glance to the form / That familiarity is tradition, and tradition is learned / That learned things are taught at times—that this form can be taught / This is a reproducible form, because it is taught and institutionalized / The other work is expected to be generated by expectations of the self towards production, a demand or mandate within to make something and to make something in a certain way / When that impulse is lyrical, the question is about the need for reproduction in comparison to the constant shifting towards a newness within the contemporaneous— every other sector appears (I am certainly wrong) to do away with out-of-date models

THE FINAL TECHNOLOGY
IN THE QUESTION OF GENRE

—Bob Perelman, *"The History of Art"*[115]

SKETCH OF THE POIEM/"WHAT IS POIETICS?"

I have taken twice now in this text to describe *danger*. In the first instance, the danger emerged from the need to speak because of the feeling of having something to say, while the second took to labeling this danger a 'danger of the lyric.' It could also be called a 'danger of the lyric *function*.' 'Of the' situates the genre/form as the site of the problem—and speaks towards the location of the problem's emergence, noted as dangerous, while the speaker or subject utilizing the form and encountering the problematic has had their complicity in the problem and its process removed, rendering them no longer solely **responsible**, but **influenced**. The lyric function is an elevated mood, of poetry, wherein people locate a formulation of what some view as a 'pure saying,' and glorify this speech against the speech of others.

The need to situate form before user, as well as form before language [the articulation of thought] in the issues derived from them is a matter of life and death—following upon and alongside Heidegger's concerns regarding the technological, as for instance about technology producing 'one-track thinking' in *What Is Called Thinking?* Technology occludes perception of the essence of ourselves. In our schema of language, we regard **genre as a technology**.

> **Genre**: gender, a form or kind.
> From **genus** or type.

This technology bears the capacities to be instructed and reproduced readily, to be taken up and used, to be occupied as a career—in manners not positive but **co-optable**, as an exploitation of pure saying towards un-real ends. As a technology, genre is empirically definable—it demands rules and structures that have rigidity and themselves define the user and their speech/speaking: in poetry, schools of poets occur in part by alignment with these rules and, the other facet of technology, poetry's *forms* which are its technological structuration. By stifling the possibility of expression through these impositions, technology inhibits our *gifted* means to come close to the 'Being of being' (or whatever terms are under consideration towards that essence).

This is not explicitly about the occupation of genre by a work of art, which involves the *inevitable translation* of a hearing of Being into an articulation, the articulation of which will necessarily be categorically generic in some form or fashion. This is instead to discuss the way in which the structure and description [definition] of genres has led to their dissemination as practicable forms outside the hearing-of-being, such for instance as that people can be somehow 'instructed' in these generic ways at the collegiate level, trained, say—in an MFA or drama program—to convincingly constantly be capable of producing generic work. The discussion of genre also enfolds the matter of generic outputs, regarded often as valuably aesthetic, against some iteration of spoken language in most day-to-day use, that that terrain of spoken language is not to be eliminated from the overall schema at play here.

At the core of the problematic lies the nature of genre as aligned with the essential impacts of technology in regards to thinking. This alignment produces an intense and ongoing (developing) concern—with a solution posited in the further elevation and recognition of the role ποίησις/ **poiesis** (emerging as and through making) plays versus a standardized image of poetry/the poetic and its death-of-thought manufactured by its technological dominion. Exegetic generic adherence—against this further preliminary in language—is simply unsatisfactory as we seek to determine the origination of works of art and how they convey our Being. We are averse to self-assertion guised as interpretation in the classic manner of exegesis for it is not involved in a speaking of Being but in an examination of what radiates from another['s] speaking of Being—which is itself located in the work of art [the technical domain involves this classic exegetical method, hosted often in the University]. Therein the interpretation seeks only to document and evidence a technological imaging of Being.

Pure saying in the work of art emerges through poiesis, after the hearing of a **poiem**—the true poietical is this product, the mediatory-remediatory poiem (which speaks and effects speech). The poiem is the impulsing form compelling production, and the poem is a medium the production occurs within—just as the visual arts, through the permeative effect of aesthetical reception, find their various forms/media functioning in the same way. We generally sketch the poiem therefore as the ideal formulation regarding the genesis of the work of art, with that the poiem is a formation in the poietical register capable of being engaged with by variable genres. It is imperative, as well, that we understand language here to have a wider array of expressions tethered to it than strictly spoken or written inscriptions. Language, when poietic, can manifest in whatever forms capable of the total range of a subject's somatic and psychical composition.

I am, thus, not completely aligned with Heidegger's thought, though [it appears] he comes closest to my thinking about form, language, and [the] production of art—for one, I reject vehemently that works constructed in a fashion devoid of poietic language and thought are useful outside of narrowly defined technical circles (think of literary criticism: who reads it and who is it written for?). I even take pause to consider whether dramatic and prose narrative writings, especially generic ones, are capable of being poietical [116]—poetry's capacity for attunement to poiesis and its speaking comes especially in the freeing of written language there from certain grammatical rules demanded by the [other] educational paradigms we are trained within, while productions such as the novel tend towards conformity with a traditional formulaic structure. [Even then, we are noting the mere unadherence of poetry grammatically despite it's other adherence to forms aforementioned....] Certainly there are formulaic poems, as I have made clear here, just as there are poietical novels and dramas: the work of Sarah Kane (*4:44 Psychosis*) in drama/Lynne Dreyer (*Tamoka*) in prose are strong examples of this—alongside transgressive-traditional generic formulations akin to circumstances such as are manifest in the prose poem. Mere presentation aligned with an expected genre—typically initiated in the mind visually (paragraphs key with prose, left justified briefer lines/non-conformity to any alignment with poetry)—causates the user (who may then deploy, becoming commentator, and, if influencing others, then mediator...) to believe that the work under examination is of that genre. But, were we to move beyond genre to the point of origin of the work of art, we could document instead this 'linguistic' register of the poietical—the poietic [linguistic] register which drives poiesis as a felt or received impulse emergent from our essential Being.

Alongside the poietic register would occur [at least] two others: the technical and the prosaic. [117] The technical and prosaic registers, situated in the commonplace [common-space], are the domain of many daily experiences—news journalism [in print and television format], instruction manuals, classroom education, work rhetoric/dialect, for some instances, and the association of these with functionality, expectation, and demand upon the subject (demands such as accruing capital in order to survive). These registers are only nominally different, their situations instead oriented towards dynamics of use [context]. Unlike the poietic register, these are also strictly manifested in spoken, written, or otherwise communicated language [sign language] bearing linguistic codification through grammar, vocabulary, and syntax. As compared to the poietical, these registers do nothing to sensate our relation to our Being—having little capacity in range to do so—

but instead define our understandings of it in strict, linear, terms believed to be total [the complete capture of an entity/ concept/theory/belief occurs *here*], causing these registers to be the terrain of technology which denies our closeness to Being, replicating it somehow in its re-production and control towards our social reality, wherein we become the Godhead of our existence and forget to contemplate the whyness of even thought. Out of this domain come the violent ills this book mapped. These are the registers which stifle our expressions of thinking whom we are, why, what we have done, and where from we emerge, while aligning us with controlling mechanisms that restrict our freedoms.

What is important here is to acknowledge that the poietical process (the construction of the work of art— guided by the impulse) has produced manifold forms. These forms can be occupied, used, or re-deployed as 'copy/ mimic/emulation' by others who populate their copy with content born from the prosaic or technical register. This leads us to the conclusion that not all poems are poietical works, and not all supposed works of art effect ecstatic immersions of our world—instead, the work of art has been bowdlerized and interpreted as *something else* than what it is. We have lost the ability to delineate the pure saying adequately when in contact with an aesthetically oriented production.

BEGINNING WITH A DEFINITION/ENDING UPON SILENCE

> Copies, *from* copia *being misleading,* abundance *suggests many affordances, but* moving backwards the dynamic is confined and contextualized—situated in the utterance—copiam describendi facere to permit to transcribe

The work of art and hollow treadings after works of art are not the same [118]—though for some recipients they may function similarly or in the same fashion. Certainly, a 'work of art' can produce energetic impulses in a recipient which call their subject *to make,* but the content of their production occurs across the widest array possible (the upper limit of the total population of humanity, considering).

Has the impulse itself become disconnected from pure-spoken productions and instead occupied a perceptual status, held subject to subject, against a standardized definition of 'art work' and 'fabricated work portending to be art'?

While this 'receipt-function' of a work of art may suggest that the matters of register here differ person to person, if that is so that is only because of the technological sprawl the discourses about the work of art have taken on. Were we to push along the lines here examined, an intervention in the praxis of thought and perception could occur—especially where we could upend the role the Institution (temporally—its historical trace and the contemporaneous inscription such effects) and the State play in the education of the speaking subject (alt-def: the inscribing subject). Those camps mandate our speech. We must continuously hold extreme caution over the nature Institutional and State influence plays in our languages, especially where we claim to hold that space as the locus of our reflection of our interior being or essence. We also have to acknowledge that control is occurring, rather than continuing to speak amidst it.

The argumentary telos of this operates towards a total societal restructuring of communicative engagement where much of the prosaic and technical material texts/works are denigrated or halted in favor of widespread poietical inscriptions. I think this is not so shocking as it initially sounds—we can generally all agree that the work of art/works of art effect immersive, ecstatic, understandings **[jouissance— ecstatic re-terraining of the understanding of the subject/Being/essence;** the poietical definition of any 'thing' is an ecstatic one, only capable of generating a total possibility of re-presentation] of the World and Being that technical, generically constrained, productions can only, if at all, graze. Consider Gertrude Stein's definition of poetry in *Lectures in America*:

> *Poetry is concerned with using with abusing, with losing with wanting, with denying with avoiding with adoring with replacing the noun. It is doing that always doing that, doing that and doing nothing but that. Poetry is doing nothing but using losing refusing and pleasing and betraying and caressing nouns. That is what poetry does, that is what poetry has to do no matter what kind of poetry it is. And there are a great many kinds of poetry.*[119]

Recalling that "A noun is a name of anything," and that "in writing prose names that is nouns are completely uninteresting." Poetry is "a state of knowing and feeling a name" in a way that is bodily and psychical, touched by eroticism, compulsion, desire, and genesis. We are aware thus of a delineation in categorical genre—prose versus poetry—about the power and capacity of saying *the thing.*

When we write about works of art, we acknowledge this power and capacity inside poetry that our writings outside it typically lack—it is then upon us to speak forth poietically if we seek to speak [of/on] Being. Speaking poietically, being a speech resultant from hearing—hearing there being a tandem conceptualization of influence and communion. [120]

WHY IS THE POET A "GENIUS"?

To not be able to speak forth [produce] poietically is *not* a deficiency. The Institution as wielded by the State deprives us of our poietical drives. The speaking subject finds such articulations discouraged, suppressed, then eradicated through their educational indoctrination. It must thus be re-learned. The educational apparatus mandates technical generic form, for careerist purposes. In the process of deprogramming these Institutional mandates, silence is inevitable. The terrain the Institution perpetuates suggests that silence is the result of incapacity, of a failure or flaw (which can not be surmounted)—

commodity driven culture and the culture of genius here intertwine to devise a pantheon of more-capable-than-others producers of works of art who are to be listened to and studied. Denise Levertov appears very keen upon the higher power of 'genius function' which some purport to belie poetry, its transmission, use, and impact. Here, we are looking at "A Common Ground" in *The Jacob's Ladder*. A denatured "authorship" is present, which Heidegger often notes in his discussions of poetry and the universal—not reflexive—tendency of the form. What author? Who? Akin to how Heidegger has described poets as 'venturesome' or 'apart' figures, her iteration is of "not [a] common speech/a dead level/but the uncommon speech of paradise,/tongue in which oracles/speak to beggars and pilgrims."

There it is, again, an elaboration that pure saying is identified as a characteristic of certain individuals. Here it is situated complexly amidst religion/destination driven by God(heads). The epigraph to the book brings us even closer toward an interpretation of the interaction of man/ Earth and god/Heaven [das Geviert] as one activated by Man ("even the ascent and descent of the angels depends on my deeds.").

Levertov's poem carefully examines capacity and condition for poetic inscription, using terms like "common" and "fine" [121] and their alternatives consistently. All people are common, some are also uncommon. The common seek pleasure or, rather, find pleasure (encounter pleasure—the text doesn't render this phrase with a subject or operator, only as a virtue or maxim), which exists in the poem—whatever 'truth' the poem conveys or impact, it is associated emotionally with positivity and so forth, leading to our use here of 'pleasure,' it is only to grasp at a better word—such as 'sustenance.' For the text found nourishes, the words are raised for a procedure analogous to consumption [the poem thus serves a purpose, and is differentiated from the/an other text]. The first section lays that out: "To reach those shining pebbles,/that soil where uncommon men/have labored in their virtue/and left a store//of seeds for a planting!" The poem's purpose is to be deployed, as the seed is to be planted. We know no content to the poem(s) conjuring this meditation on the poem itself, only a gestalt relation to the scope or canon of poetic language in totality.

The second section almost shows us that the demands of a capitalist society (life in the United States) lead us to a reliance on poietic/uncommon speech [for therapeutic reasons] where these poems are impacting us during our technical/quotidian dynamics, as with "poems stirred/into paper coffee cups [...] and the traffic grinding the/borders of spring—entering/human lives forever." We mean this to say that the second section suggests, but not outright speaks upon, the reason for a distinction in the voice of humans that some of us speak uncommonly[/poietically] and some of us speak commonly[/technically]. Perhaps, for some, this awareness occurs more maximally in this section because of the grandiosity with which the poem and its [lyrical] language are described ("to speak as the sun's/ deep tone of May gold speaks") which juxtaposes against the brief descriptions of people here.

But, the closest we can come to a critique or a "why" for the genius capacity is veiled—the speaker (the author) is not making this critical step. They only appear to know of it as a radiating circumstance, a victim themselves of the systemic deprivation of "uncommon" language once in actuality widely common: "men/in business suits awkwardly/recline" amidst the cosmic rays the poem(s) are tracing as they dimensionally grid this conceptual city.

We live awkwardly in such uniforms of the expectations of us—expectations which run antithetical to the nature of choice and will/willing. Conducting our lives in this way, adhered as we choose to be or are forced to be to the systems and institutions which dominate our lives, we are compelled into awkward postures of incapacity: we simply cannot, at least not maximally, "Be." The deprivation of the sensation and sighting of Being occurs as the mandatory commons is compulsed by these institutions, by States, by technology. These forces then craft the cruel illusion of an idea of uncommonality [the fabricated poiesis [122]] to therapize disdain and disillusionment, as with a speaking subject's felt incapacity or frustration with their speech capacity. It is generally easier to construct a dynamic where geniuses and special bodies—bodies whose genius has time and time failed to be proven in the genesis of what is regarded as genius (the essential question, in language, "why different?" posed as "why are they a poet and not myself?")—exist in difference than it is 'easy' for us to operate within a destructed and revolutionary framework that is murky, inviable, and invisible within our current system.

So, this itself devolves into a "writing about the work of art," no? Absconding with such exegetical matter and returning to our matter of 'study,' we suggest that this study can [and does, as aesthetic 'influence' suggests] occur preferentially poietically and not technically—the study within the dynamic of poietic hearing undergoes a transition within the poietical state (of which much remains to be said) into the *re-mediation,* however that occurs [or, in whatever form]. This is because within the study of the poietical work, **study** here being the true hearing of Being that is brought forth in that work (and not a mere self-assertive interpretation of the work), the transition into the new state of Being has occurred—the **transformation.** [123] So, the study results not in interpretations but transmutations [deployments] (or at least it should)—which are on their face perceivable and capable of being read also as 'new outputs' affording their own poietical encounter[s]; all this creating a chain of mediation/re-mediation (with the works being mediatory re-mediations). This is the study I propose.

Finally, we pay homage to the silence encountered by those of us who produced 'study' in a technical register and find themselves within the proposed schema incapable of hearing poietical impulses and feeling their manifest forms. In terms of those 'suffering' this condition of silence during the upheaval in the societal transition back [for it is *back*, for reasons beyond this space] to the primary poietical state of inscription, the amelioration to anxiety surrounding the silence—a post-traumatic stress of the capitalist drive to make, speak, create, and control the definition of reality and Being—is prescribed to be: *awaiting*—listening for—the hearing of Being.

NOTES

1. https://wikileaks.org/vault7/document/EXTENDING_User_Guide/EXTENDING_User_Guide.pdf

2. *The EXTENDING implant can be installed using a Close Access method. The EXTENDING installer is loaded onto a USB stick. This USB stick is then inserted into the target SAMSUNG F Series TV, and the installer is run.*

3. https://www.dni.gov/index.php/features/bin-laden-s-bookshelf

4. https://www.dni.gov/files/documents/ubl2017/english/Letter%20to%20sister%20Um%20Abd-al-Rahman.pdf

5. [it is a fabrication of this medium, co-opted to exploit users]

6. Termed by some **Trump Derangement Syndrome** which *does* afflict a neoliberal [and not universally *leftist*] milieu—pernicious in its domineering over (the Institute that is long become) Poetryland USA. The members of this faction are [at times] coincidentally out of lock-step with the necessary (PACBI-adjacent) boycotts ongoing [against this (criminal) genocide], as in this poetry landscape where major (often become commercial-academic institutional) figures such as Rae Armantrout have published in consent manufacturing outlets such as *The Atlantic* (whose editor-in-chief is a former IOF prison guard, Jeffery Goldberg [thanks to Joe Hall for his research on Armantrout's complicit

blind participation with Zionism and its manufacture as is published in his contribution to ISSUE 01 through my own Blue Bag Press]) while also sharing false/untrue memes and information on Facebook about the election in their concerned bemoaning of the possibilities of a second Trump administration in the then of "the waning" or obviously losing capacity of the Democrat presidential campaign-corporation. There *is* a responsibility, first of all, for the producer of culture to interrogate the venue they seek to platform their productions—residual effects are damaging, and oversight can prove either associational or dramatically induce complicity. There is here present also the marker of desire for a publication, some career desire—many of these venues are considered amongst the best—which is placed ahead of necessary political labor. If the figures culpable here are, as I suggest they are, major players in the contemporary poetry scene, they are also not figures who one would associate lack of critical thinking skills with, meaning this political labor is being entirely ignored and overlooked alongside the voices who promote such labor—usually figures from the oppressed classes and groups. This is an old story.

Now, *The Atlantic* has neoliberal guardian-coverage (alt-def: security) because Jeffrey Goldberg was 'inadvertently' included in a government defense thread on Signal. Such elevates them into a heroic position for many, and leads to further oversight of these prior insidious engagements. I am concerned that certain perceivably useful, moral, or ethical actions and choices by otherwise wildly complicit bodies—especially in a scaled fashion towards the more spectacular orientations of such possibilities—could lead to too-wide societal forgetting, not forgiveness, of the same actors' prior complicity. There is, yes, a need to recognize growth and change, but also to—not even in a historiographical manner—reckon with prior actions or lack thereof, as here where this occurs within an urgently recent violent dynamic. I therefore think of the body which abided—sleeping—and 'woke' still is as asleep. Remains so. No matter the dispositional apparence of sympathies towards the global minoritized subject(s), the neoliberal body is a nationalist body typically only awake to domestic devastations rendering upon their selves 'exigent' plights while international crises similarly fold in in usually posterior fashion and in relation to domestic insecurity. Only demonstrable action—on the(ir) way to left-ism—can repair, in the eyes of the left-which-seeks-solidarity from these parties and constantly winds up empty-handed.

Armantrout in the Summer of 2024 complained that her own neoliberal commentating on social media had led to back-lash, as on her Facebook page with roughly 3500 friends. So-cial media has proved a valuable tool during the *OINTMENT WEATHER* project for analyzing the global sociopolitical concerns and other political dynamics absent in the published writing of certain authors, affording a venue to see political af-filiations and ideologies which a book or other publication may only vaguely gesture at. At the time of these postings, Arman-trout had recently stated that she, too, disapproved of the events in the Middle East, but supported Biden's policies towards the environment when advocating that Biden remain on the Demo-cratic ticket during the tumultuous weeks during which Biden's campaign collapsed under widespread pressures. Armantrout's environmental concerns are no surprise to close readers of her work and her public comments about it: she has more recently written a good deal about her grandchildren and obviously wants to know there is a world still for them, holding concern for what such a world may look like. It has thus been unfortunate that her views and actions have not for some time consistently also applied in an inscribed fashion to the children in Gaza, whose future is uncertain after the violent (and ecologically devastating) destruction of their homeland as funded and endorsed enthusiastically by the same President she endorsed.

Further in alignment with this neoliberal political problematic is the portion of Armantrout's memoir *True* wherein she relates a brief, but insightful biographical narrative and analysis of familial race-hate in the United States: *One instance of* [my parents'] *racism particularly shocked me. We were driving through the park on Highway 395* (now 163) *when the car in front of us was sideswiped and sent tumbling off the road to land upside down in a gully. I was upset and wanted to help, but my parents said they were "only Negroes."* Regardless the usage of "racism" to ascribe an identity or perceptual framework upon the parents prior, only sentences later does Armantrout declare *I don't want to give the wrong impression here. My parents weren't obsessed with the race issue: they weren't Klan members or White supremacists in an organized way. They didn't hate African-Americans; they simply assumed their inferiority without giving it much thought.* (Atelos, 2010. Page 26). I aver these follow-up claims create a sequence of contradictions leading to a declaration of racism defined as an alignment with "organization" and institutionality and not as an insidious always already occurring state of human nature or being—slightly ironic considering the otherwise sketched State alignments the same author holds, and here showing the neoliberal fallacy that problematics exist but within the 'other' Institution or 'other side,' and not in the root of the national structure and function intrinsically. Armantrout also conducts this amidst historical reflection—as with the correction of the highway number—which does not also carry contemporized racial awareness—that her parents were not Klan members is a backwards temporality of the event described and not carried forward to the time of the new highway number: why is only the minute detail worth chronological clarification? Armantrout's parents *were* obsessed with the race issue in their violent dismissal of the potentially injured party. The mechanism of the later sentences in tandem with the temporalization in this excerpt function as defensive maneuvers to elide a disgusting and indefensible act within the author's world. The author is seeking a means to defend it.

However, while the racial question evoked by Armantrout's statements in *True* persists, we must also take a pause to recognize another shift. On March 21st, 2025, following the nomination that week of her *Go Figure* for a PEN America Voelcker award, Armantrout announced her nomination on Facebook, garnering just under 30 innocuous likes, with Elaine Equi congratulating her in a comment. Over the following three days, Armantrout made the following comments on her post: 1) *But I've also learned the protest/boycott against PEN is still active* 2) *I tried to post something about a picket line but it was blocked* 3) *Anyone have thoughts about PEN's responsibility re annihilation of Gaza? Should I withdraw my book? PLEASE only answer this if you actually know me* 4) *PS I find the bombing atrocious. My question is about PEN's role and responsibility* and 5) *I guess no one will touch this question. Third rail???* By the final comment, we arrive at Monday, the 24th of March, 2025, and we should note as we do so that, as mentioned above, researching the institutions and venues one associates themselves with is vital—in this case that research is being conducted, though it *is* partially outsourced despite fairly readily available source work.

At this point, having tracked the unfolding conversation over the prior days, and noting the return of a semi-habitual tendency of Armantrout's to enact a censorious moderation of her large Facebook page towards only actual friends/acquaintances/colleagues, I wondered about the possibility for intervention. I contacted Ry Cook, a mutual friend and ardent advocate for the boycotts and wider action for Gaza and global liberations, and sent the thread. I implored Ry to see what they could do. Gratefully, Ry posted the WAWOG boycott page with a succinct comment that, while Armantrout had the right to her choice, this is why they align with PACBI initiatives. Armantrout followed up that day that she had withdrawn the book from consideration.

After some further consideration, I followed up with Rae via a comment that this was a moving and vital action, and thanked her, as others did, for this choice. At the same time, and considering the viral status that Brendan Shimoda's open letter withdrawing his title from award consideration had had (in the 2025 cycle), I encouraged her—if she could—to make a public statement expressing her why for the action. Regardless if she does this, so long as it is true that she has joined the boycott, we must acknowledge the nature of change and the use of voice at hand. I am grateful for this barometric relief. I had previously structured the commentary here to make direct reference to a number of other established poets, their social media and otherwise commentaries, and continue the indictment of neoliberalism further. However, the motivation of the commentary is not invective laden polemic, but urgent imploring towards the culturally established neoliberal poet to *do the work* necessary to make the changes which will actually impact wider awarenesses and radical actions. This is, simply, a discussion of tension between neoliberal and leftist camps, and our leftist need for the neoliberal to largely abandon their predilections and poorly thought through beliefs, so close and adherent to American Empire, in order for them to come with us in the march to a revolution against not only the contemporary Administration and its egregious acts—acts so egregious many of the neoliberal poets are shedding their past ideations—but the whole insidious history of this nation, a reservoir of capitalism, white supremacy, and systemic, violent oppression against any bodies living outside its heralded somatic-cultural paradigm pulsing out of the cancerous organ of State elevated cis-whiteness and individualistic wealth accrual.

7. Which is impossible despite the 'education' in the humanities and cultural studies that the left pretends they hold and learn from.

8. The lines in question: *But this relief made no more sense than the news with its endless stories about suicide bombs, but never anything about the reasons why the suicide bombs were happening. When they watched the news, they could easily think that people were spontaneously blowing themselves up for no reason.*

Spahr, Juliana. *The Transformation.* Atelos 2007, 160.

9. *With a wink the nations are informed that peace is the elimination of war, but that meanwhile this peace which eliminates war can be secured only by war. Against this war-peace in turn we launch a peace offensive whose attacks can hardly be called peaceful. War—the securing of*

peace; and peace—the elimination of war. How is peace to be secured by what it eliminates? Something is fundamentally out of joint here… Heidegger, Martin. *What Is Called Thinking?* Harper Perennial, 2004. 83.

Elimination from e+limin or threshold[ing (with a verb capacity)] *then* eliminat- or *turned out from the threshold, the doors.* Elimination is inseparable from cultural separations, homogenizations, and racialisms.

10. David Covucci via https://brobible.com/life/article/osama-bin-laden-porn-collection-foia/

11. Peter Holley quoting David Corvucci via https://www.washingtonpost.com/news/post-nation/wp/2015/06/10/a-bro-asked-the-cia-about-osama-bin-ladens-porn-stash-the-agency-answered/

12. Quoted via https://www.reuters.com/article/wikileaks-stratfor-idUSL5E8DR0120120227/

13. *Devastation is more unearthly than destruction. Destruction only sweeps aside all that has grown up or been built up so far; but devastation blocks all future growth and prevents all building. Devastation is more unearthly than mere destruction. Mere destruction sweeps aside all things including even nothingness, while devastation on the contrary establishes and spreads everything that blocks and prevents. The African Sahara is only one kind of wasteland. The devastation of the earth can easily go hand in hand with a guaranteed supreme living standard for man, and just as easily with the organized establishment of a uniform state of happiness*

for all men. Devastation can be the same as both, and can haunt us everywhere in the most unearthly way—by keeping itself hidden. Devastation does not just mean a slow sinking into the stands. Devastation is the high-velocity expulsion of Mnemosyne [memory]. Heidegger, Martin. *What Is Called Thinking?* Harper Perennial, 2004. 29-30.

14. *In the digital encoding of the animated world, there is no wind, not even a simulated wind, but only an algorithm to simulate the appearance of wind passing through fur. [...] the digital can offer only a muted creativity; it can produce nothing truly new, but only rearrange the forms it is given.*

Evens, Aden. "Ontology of the Digital" in *The Digital and its Discontents.* Minnesota, 2024. 93.

15. Which we additionally must remember is manufactured by humans upon other humans. There is no natural order to the suffering of humans in the world today.

16. See the final chapter for a definition of technology in this context.

17. Armantrout, Rae. *Conjure.* Wesleyan, 2020. 84.

18. Not-so trivial semantics to where you may wonder about a previous footnote about Armantrout, but I proffer another Facebook posting from October 3rd, 2024, by James Sherry. Discussing editing the manuscript of *Tens,* a forthcoming project I have delighted in hearing from Kit about for some time, Sherry notes that the word processor he is using desperately wants to amend the line "No self without an other" to "No self without another."

19. [A] *performative utterance will, for example, be in a peculiar way hollow or void if said by an actor on the stage, or if introduced in a poem, or spoken in soliloquy. This applies in a similar manner to any and every utterance—a sea-change in special circumstances. Language in such circumstances is in special ways—intelligibly—used not seriously, but in ways parasitic upon its normal use—ways which fall under the doctrine of the etiolations of language. All this we are excluding from consideration. Our performative utterances, felicitous or not, are to be understood as issued in ordinary circumstances.* Austin, J.L. *How to Do Things with Words.* Oxford, 1962. 22.

20. See 'Ghost Robotics' and 'Ghost Robotics cont.' in *TUPELO IS A GENUS OF DECIDUOUS TREE.*

21. From: https://www.bellingcat.com/resources/how-tos/2021/08/26/the-telltale-traces-of-the-us-militarys-new-bladed-missile-r9x/

22. The river has since been "allowed to run wild again" (various sources) by the removal of all dams—few sources reporting this development months later brought up the fish kill here discussed only months prior. Perhaps it is true that an abundance of farmed fish were cultivated to the fry stage and beyond, but this seems suspect considering the otherwise present strains upon the food system. If there is the means to manufacture affordances for disaster, accident, error—to have extra—then there should be a means of disseminating the surplus to ensure wider access to food.

23. From: https://digitallibrary.un.org/record/3905159?ln=en

24. A new horizon being South America, which *Newseek* described [specifically, Peru] as "America's Backyard" here: https://www.newsweek.com/china-news-xi-megaport-chancay -warships-1985770

25. *The light has escaped me and now the window will fill.* Coolidge, Clark. *The Crystal Text.* The Figures, 1986. 10.

26. *the light transmits color as a scene. What then is a window.* Hejinian, Lyn. *My Life.* Burning Deck, 1980. 63.

27. *...windows are painted into air//which carries windows into your lungs, your blood, your brain.* Swensen, Cole. *The Glass Age.* Alice James Books, 2007. 6.

28. See the chapter "Park-Life."

29. The first available episode on Spotify of the controversial recent pop-cultural phenomena Hailey Welch's *Talk Tuah* includes discussion of this:

> Whitney Cummings: *Well, what's the point of memorizing any history? because we've now learned that none of it was true.*
>
> Hailey Welch: *Half of it.*
>
> Cummings: *When I grew up, I don't know if this is even what you learned in school, I learned that the Native Americans and the Pilgrims had a fun dinner.*
>
> Welch: *That's what I got for it.*
>
> [...]

Cummings: *I think the most history until now has kind of been gossip. I mean, it's kind of just, like, you know what I mean?*

Jamie Forster: *Well, I feel like if I want to battle, I'd be like, [I am] going to tell this story [...] I'm also going to say like my opponent was fat and stupid. Like, I'm going to add an insult to it too.* [1:56 - 2:50]

30. Ponge, Francis. *The Power of Language*. California University Press, 1979. 158.

31. So [this] fact is as event?

32. A government body that spent $100,000 on coffee makers, including a nearly $30,000 model for the Speaker's office. The cost of an intercept by the Iron Dome is $70,000 (this number is debated—I found a middle of the road estimate at 75k, while higher numbers are reported in Wikipedia for the cost of Tamir missiles at 100k, while the provided Axios link bottoms out at 50k—make of it what you will, the United States alone has spent so many billions on this technology in the past decade while they have provided substantially less than that across the board to all services and individuals in Gaza in the same period in time, despite the substantially reduced costs infrastructure and capacity there—this is imperialist capitalism 101. Per the reports from Israel's government, they are unable to readily defend themselves without the support of the world, and yet they can readily afford a coffee maker that costs ⅓ that of national defense against revolutionary incursion. While corruption is rampantly discussed about neighboring Lebanon, similar reports about Lebanon's parliament expenditures on

high-end or "luxury" equipment is not readily reported in the numerous exposes about that country.

33. Russ texts from Atlanta the next morning:

In your poem, I'm curious about the meta-framing that positions the reader as a demented 80yo. Is the idea that Golan is so repulsive that we'll anchor into memories of her, even when much else is long forgotten?

I think extensively throughout my reply, which includes in part the statement:

I revised the poem. Originally it did not open with the scene setting newspaper and garden elements, it started "Knesset: yesterday" and I went back and structured it as a story that is received or remembered. I received the news of Golan's speech and existence through a friend, and I want it to be remembered decades from now. I wanted to utilize the dementia symbol (syncretic time that is happening all at once with chaotic consequences to sequencing) to build that up as well. Having been concerned my work was too expository and losing poetic grounding, there is also that the narrative around the real facts pushes the essay tone away and reframes it as poetic, and I'm currently working out of the essay language in my mind and back to the poetic language incorporating facts.

I also discussed my intention to frame that sequence in the work as **offensive** and **violent** / That I want to find a way to offend

May Golan—which seems impossible / But, that **offensive** is a structure born from **offendere** breeding ground for pre- fix **offens-** (struck against) / So, there ("their") is so- matic or psychical flinching after a distressive event but there is also a planned attack upon a po- sition, a strike against / in tandem withal — these ap- pear the articles of / a horizon of war

34. **re-** & **tomare** it is [utterance::NHPRITCHARD ut ter ance] to take back to turn back

35. Thriambos / Bacchus hymn / **Etymological Poem** / Font consistency / It is not a thrombosis / *por ejemplo* / Speaking dictionary talkback etymological dictionary—I am this / Let me tell you about Semele /

Του Κάδμου η κόρη, η Σεμέλη, στο Δία γέννησε γιο λαμπρό, σαν έσμιξε ερωτικά μαζί του, τον πολύτερπνο Διόνυσο, έναν αθάνατο η θνητή. Μα τώρα και οι δυο είναι θεοί Can you see she is part of the masculine his-tory, his narrative? Mother to / Mother of / **Mother** / Is not "her"

36. *That's Mary Manning Howe Adams in The Cambridge Holmes for Liars.* Howe, Susan. *Concordance.* New Directions, 2020. 27.

37. *ANTIKYTHERA.* Antiphony Press, 2024. np.

38. Pritchard, N H. *The Matrix. Poems: 1960-1970.* Ugly Duckling/Primary Information, 2021. 3.

39. Sovereign citizens at times use the term "quantum grammar" for a similar concept corralled into a hyper-politicized right wing ideation.

40. Transchronological teleportation?

41. *Public opinion today cherishes the the notion that the thinking of thinkers must be capable of being understood in the same way as the daily newspaper. That all men cannot all follow the thought processes of modern theoretical physics is considered quite in order.*

Heidegger, Martin. *What Is Called Thinking?* 238-9.

42. Two of his animal outlines from the book comprise an unfinished tattoo cuff on my ankle

43. fabrication? It is hard to discern the division in terminology here. The bottomline is the critical fober behind the making.

44. My first book, *BESPOKE*, concludes with a forty page, total erasure poem of Joanne Kyger's *All This Every Day*. Erased public domain texts included the books of Genesis and Exodus ("Fourth Order") and "Hymn to Intellectual Beauty" ("Hymn"). *ANTIKYTHERA* includes an erased portion, this time in blackout style, from *As I Lay Dying*.

45. *my eye joining the two in a / simple surgery* Jena Osman writes on page 50 of *The Character*.

46. [M]useum [C]opy

47. As pre-installed (bundled) font on Google Docs, though it remains on MS Word.

48. Do we even have the time to contemplate—hurtling forward always as we are—that Google is *so large* a corporation both by employment and economic stake that 'human rights' is

a fundamental concern not only of its corporate ideology but its influence? The technological purchase in the legislation and dominion of 'rights' or their stakehood is inherently driven by this aspect of influence.

49. A concept which we regard in its perceptual and inscribed form—as an illusory discourse manufactured by governments and forces of States or State-aligned bodies, who themselves are the primary venue where rights, human and otherwise, are dispensed and controlled

50. These are, again, critically important in being understood not as *actual* rights, but dispensations of 'rights' controlled by a government. This portrayal of dispensation is not meant to capture the actual situation about equity and rights in contemporary American society—it would not effectively do so regardless, for the entire portrayal is meant itself to map the near cinematic production in terms of control and manipulation the dispensation of rights, as a spectacle, involves.

51. which is also a functionary of the temporal relation of the corporation within the *public-political* discourse about rights at the governmental level, such that Google bears a trajectorial overlay with more acceptable commentaries on sexual inclusion in an era in which people neglected civil rights surrounding race in the way they consider them today, with the increase of a renewed civil rights discourse surrounding race which has grown since the 2010s

52. This chapter was composed prior to the Federal Government's destruction of many DEI programs, grants, funds, and

protocols in the first weeks of the second Trump administration. The ready capacity for such 'programs' removal should give us concern about the nature of their implementation in the past. This is part of a larger systemic failure on liberal legislator's parts wherein fundamental matters of rights are only legislated piecemeal or through Executive power. Even passed legislation is tenuous in its permanence. Future legislation has to be more permanent, such as through constitutional emendation.

53. Google's parent company, Alphabet, was created to offset substantial operations from Google as a corporation, creating the illusion of separation between the firms in attempting to prevent the ongoing threat of antitrust action by the government. Google has continued to be the persistent target of antitrust efforts since the formation of Alphabet, as recently as March 8th, 2024, in this report by Reuters. Japanese regulators have launched an antitrust suit against Alphabet, while Russian authorities revoked financial assets from the corporation, forcing them (the business entity "Google Russia") into bankruptcy within the country. Issues alleged by the Russian Federation come down to Google's not censoring pro-Ukrainian materials/anti-war commentary across its various platforms, such as Gmail and Youtube. United States complaints in antitrust suits often have revolved around Google's apparent intentional censoring and manipulation of search results on google.com. The discrepancy between the actions on either side speaks into the corporation's values towards capital accrual by any means necessary, often operating along contradictory lines depending on the disposition of the State in the governing territory.

54. This section had not intended to devolve as such into the broadside against Google, but is inevitably informed by having read, the evening I composed much of the Google material, just prior, Jena Osman's 2014 title *Corporate Relations* (Burning Deck) wherein is examined rhetorically, legalistically, and archivally, concerns about the State and its exertions judicially over the person—as a subject (human) and as a body (corporation). Osman documents SCOTUS in the origin point of preserving and protecting corporatocracy here. *How could our Constitution* [does the pairing of "our" with the specific document type necessitate, grammatically, the proper noun form?] *protect corporations as if they were "of the people"? But the fact is, corporations have been collecting a variety of Constitutional* [appropriate proper noun] *rights since 1886* (74) and that *the courts* [...] *created corporations as persons, gave birth to corporations as persons* (25). Elsewhere, she writes *The framers knew full well / whose right of subjacent support had been withheld or waived* (45), while close readings of the poems "Hale vs Henkel" and "Marshall vs Barlow's" will demonstrate Osman's structuring of a court flaunting or ignoring the "framing of the document," with the particular concern that the originary point of the document was somehow against capital accrual, itself buried in the associative bridge between the sequence of lines *the minds of the framers / compelling a man to be a witness against himself / look behind the corporate form and discover* (32, emphasis added). I may disagree ultimately with some of Osman's conclusions as aligned with the nature of the State overall and a possibility of recuperation amidst them, but the system at play is an incredibly effective reading in lines of corporate critique and

historiography of the corporate class, while also embodying the valuable re-mediatory position of a poietic articulation (as is discussed in the final chapter of this volume).

55. Osman, Jenna. *Motion Studies.* Ugly Duckling Presse, 2019. 44.

56. O'Hara, Frank. "Saint Paul and all that" in *The Lunch Poems.* City Lights, 2014. 51

57. Tape similarly intrigues. Tape also derives from an Old English term tæppe being a narrow strip (thus matching *form*) while others connect, also, to the Middle Low German tapen, itself being "to pluck or tear" and thus a syncretism of antipositonal acts, connection and separation, formulating what is a word denoting a dynamic which "brings together."

58. EDITOR'S NOTE: this was written months prior to the disturbing technological attacks conducted by Israel upon Hezbollah fighters in Lebanon, including remote detonation of pagers and walkie-talkies

59. https://jalaltoufic.com/downloads/Jalal_Toufic,_(Vampires),_An_Uneasy_Essay_on_the_Undead_in_Film_(mid_res).pdf page 129

60. Reported in an Al Jazeera live feed March 19, 2024

61. Shortly after writing this, I plate up dinner which had sat in the oven baking as I worked on it. My husband went out to check the mail and came back with what he described as *all junk mail.* One envelope is from Joe Biden for President, and the enclosed fundraising missive tells me *You know we're better than this*

62. https://www.aljazeera.com/news/2024/3/19/indias-rahul-gandhi-ends-unity-march-with-huge-election-rally-in-mumbai

63. Terminology is here derived/co-opted from Joan Retallack's "Essay as Wager" in *The Poethical Wager.*

64. *Epicurus posited the swerve* (a.k.a clinamen) *to explain how change could occur in what early atomists saw as composed of elemental bodies moving in unalterable paths. Epicurus attributed the redistribution of matter that creates noticeable differences to the sudden zig or zag of rogue atoms.* (Retallack, Joan. *The Poethical Wager.* Wesleyan, 2002. 2)

65. Epicurus, Letter to Herodotus.

66. Butler, Judith. *Gender Trouble.* Routledge, 2007. 96.

67. Editor's note: Author stops, takes break and plays Mario Wonder for a little while. Mario games are recently emerging as digital mechanisms for alleviating depression per various reports on the game Mario Odyssey. Author's husband is disabled with severe treatment resistant depression. The game appears to moderately improve initial feelings of sadness during the day when he interacts with it. Author then wonders about the nerfing of Princesses Peach and Daisy in the universe of *Mario* and the perpetuation of sexist ideologies within such minimally narrated games.

68. Salah, Trish. *Lyric Sexology, Vol I.* Roof Books, 2014. 9.

69. Tardos, Anne. *Cat Licked The Garlic*. Tsunami Editions, 1992. 1.

70. ibid.

71. ibid. 12

72. Darragh, Tina. "Don't Face Off the Fractals" in *Jimmy and Lucy's House of K #4*. 5-12.

73. *Eventually, the invention leapt from the monitoring of private space to surveilling public space, all in the name of security. A bank of monitors, with a single guard (a "force multiplier"). [...] In the 1990s, digital technology made it easier to record and store images, which led to a rapid increase in the use of the cameras. [...] Half a century* [after the patenting of the CCTV] *millions of CCTVs, connected via satellite, scan various populations across the world as they go about their business.* (Osman, Jena. *Motion Studies*. Ugly Duckling Presse, 2019. 44). To which I append on the notion of this "business" people are afoot, *labor labors to escape / its end* (Pearson, Ted. *Encryptions*. Singing Horse Press, 2007. 34.)

74. *from party favors / to party discipline— / who's your daddy?* (ibid., 31).

75. Homo economicus / *trades on denizens / increasingly inured / to the wholesale price / of rank immiseration— / spanning the antipathies / of* have and not / *the exchange rate apparently / favors the sacral / smoke that rises / from their hovels* (ibid, 41).

76. Darragh, Tina. *Dream Rim Instructions*. Drogue Press, 1999. 15.

77. This chapter is dedicated to Rachel Lauren Myers and Alex Tretbar, who provided invaluable insights without which I would have not been able to finish it. Thank you both for your inspirations as well.

78. Swensen, Cole. *Ours*. University of California Press, 2008. 7.

79. Clifford, Pat and Tyrone Williams. *washpark*. delete press. 2021. 4.

80. FIRST FACTS

These parks were constructed for the divine royalty of France and have been, in temporal descent, 'liberated' into the commons—at least, that's the general perception outlined historiographically. The copy for the front flap of *Ours* describes this transition as ironic—suggesting a liberalism as to the way the park-space is regarded—because the designer of these parks, Andre Le Nôtre, has a last name meaning 'ours.' This is a substantial point of departure critics reacting to Swensen's book have taken up, as this is an outright tenuous and romantic connection to history, which renders the historical towards incoherence and falsification as only partial facticity (**selective memory**)—this is a condition of modernity, especially amidst the technological dissemination of near *all* information. The front flap is derived from the author's note preceding the text. That author's note disputes the role of the text historically, or, as historiography. *That story*, Swensen writes of the life of Le Nôtre and this French historical time, *and others inform some of the following poems, but none of them is necessary, or even particularly helpful, for reading the poems themselves.* (*Ours*. xi). Of concern amongst the same pages here as well would be the line *A garden is a sequence that has no basis in fact* (20).

I suggest this denial of facticity for the reader—or, a loosening of the need for facts—begets itself out of a precedent tendency of oversight predicated on a white-historical (art historical; see the "Site Visit" in "Antitrust") worldview for one which has the audacity (afforded by its somatic capacities) to ignore historical information, especially relevant to a violent colonial and imperial society such as France. History for this producer is a terrain of selections out of which the producer may enhance their aesthetic intention, rather than an urgent experience through whose signs and impressions the body experiences their life as *lived under*. The same denial of historicization, that the poems can be read outside knowledge or history, exacerbates the contemporization of the poems in this volume—leading us to a further situation in which we analogize today against the past and see [or, are forced to see only] a positive connection as outlined by Swensen. I do not believe this is a debatable concept. *Ours* leads us to 2007, where the park scene in question is regarded as problematized not because of outright social conditions and oppressive dynamics, but instead for ecological destruction: *The rue d'Assas has cut off the entire northwest sector, and half the trees are gone./ The other half have unconscionably grown.* (ibid. 53). This and the mention on page 75 of 'time traveling historians' positively insert the aristocratic class (this occurs at least twice in the text with Marie Antoinette) as trace memory nostalgically recalling the origination of these specific parks (we also recall that **the park** is by no means defined in Swensen's work because there are not any contacts with other parks in other societies—the park in her 1991 work *Park* is unqualified in any specific detail tethering it to any geography or time frame outside vague modifiers, and, most essentially, the producer)[I would presume the park in *Park* is in the United States].

In contrast, Williams and Clifford's text was composed beginning as far back as 2009, roughly within the social-conditional parameters of Swensen's. Yet, the collaborators elected to interview people who lived near the park (which is almost 200 years old), as well as spend endless observational time amongst the space—they did not simply walk through, but cared. They had also educated themselves, apparently, in sociopolitical theories and causes related to the suffering of those living adjacent to such municipal spaces. Or else, it is simply sufficient that they are aware of how life is *Spelled out quietly by the generous population of a mixed neighborhood abstracted from mixed identities in lieu of proper names, common property. A passion for the decrepit in lieu of propriety. (washpark. 3).* The rise of a new era of slavery, in the French Colonial Empire, coincided with the life of Andre Le Nôtre—*Le code noir* was passed in 1685 by the same king who employed Le Nôtre: Louis XIV (the code dictated conditions and practices regarding slavery and for free people of color in a society where slavery had been concurrent with ongoing colonial/Imperial expansion, though regulated by land owners and local authorities up to this point more than by the French State). This despite Swensen claiming [in her response to the *PoemTalk* episode "Where the real exceeds the ideal"] a different time of more racial peace during the period of her project's analysis. How neither colonialism nor slavery are mentioned in any of this discourse by Swensen about this society is baffling unless you take into account the relationship this selective mentality has with history and power. Elsewhere, the ramifications of slavery trickle down onto certain residents surrounding Washington Park to this day—and this nation (the United States) will likely never give necessary reparations.

Regarding the historical social condition, Swensen asserts that *In saying that 'Spaces like this are not open,' [Ann] Seaton is actually not correct. Contemporary French society has profound problems with racism and equal access to higher education, employment, and political participation, but—again with painful irony—the former pleasure grounds of the aristocracy, with the exceptions of the few that are still in private hands, are open to everyone. There is sometimes a fee, and they are not all accessible by public transport, but no one asks your name at the gate, and no one is denied* ("Cole Swensen responds" in *Jacket2*). There are several concerns one could pick up regarding interpreting this statement. For one, the extensive qualification of the initial statement made by Swensen in her rebuttal—the parks are open *but* only if you meet this or this condition. Considering as well the lack of inclusion of minoritized bodies—especially the violently oppressed and the unhoused (as in contemporary French or American society), across the majority of Swensen's work—it actually remains to be seen whether she is capable of recognizing that 'no one is denied' without such perception issuing out of bias.

Swensen's response (as in the prefatory note to *Ours*) attempts to raise the merger of the historical condition and the contemporary condition, related to access, as though in the spirit of 'twisting free' by means of a classical Marxist rending of the means of production from the owners to the laborers (the park's transition from private to public as antithesis to the closure of land/space from the public in the park's construction). But, this is a superficial, again romantic, view of history. What is 'left out' (**excluded, unseen, or unknown?**) of the conversation is impossible to ignore. It is again also noted that the contemporary, especially the matter of homelessness, is unaddressed—ironic today considering the French government in the past has sequestered unhoused crack addicts in the Éole Gardens and forcibly displaced thousands of unhoused French residents for the 2024 Olympics. Yes, these take place after *Ours* was published, but these are decidedly not *new* State behaviors—anti-homeless sentiments have only increased alongside legislation and hostile architecture across much of the Western world where housing crises are occurring in lieu of actual solutions which rehabilitate communities in this ongoing time.

Such a claim that 'no one is denied' admittance does not reflect whether people are actually comfortable and safe in these spaces, and it outright ignores the matter of these housing crises—one could say that the park is a space of comfort for housed people who *do not want to see* the unhoused there (and the issue of housing is so pivotal, we *have* to address it). And, the lack of public transportation to public spaces is further overlooked where it is a symptom of a larger social condition of disconnection and non-access faced by people dependent on public infrastructure, which includes not only the unhoused but the disabled, low income, and elderly. In lieu of social conditions such as this, Swensen complained that the episode of *PoemTalk* did not include discussion of textual content such as the *geometry as a whole, and with it, perspective, subject positioning, and the constitution of collective subjectivity.* In fact, all of those are addressed when orienting the text towards social conditions—then or now—for the very deployment of geometric organization as was conducted in the design of the parks for the aristocracy is a component of a wider, Enlightenment thinking that came from the especially privileged and was oriented towards social controls (**grand design**)—this in a society where the monarch is vested with absolute authority as a god among humans and their power cannot be questioned.

There is not space here to so intensely rebut the totality of Swensen's claims—though hers, to use her own term as applied to Seaton, is a "very particular agenda" dedicated to preserving a production and aesthetic energy that has been critiqued for its paucity of social awareness. These linkages seem somehow vital in further honing our awareness of the relation of aesthetical production to the preservation of (or alignment with) institutions and systems which dictate the social conditions experienced by all bodies—from the privilege of those affiliated with power (in this project, specifically the white Body, or the American 'patriot' citizen 'functioning to success' in this capitalist society) to the oppression of those spectrally excised and distanced from power and its center.

81. Let us note what parks are valued and by whom—who sees and considers them, the how of this sight. If a body has totally ignored the suffering of others, they will be unfamiliar with the

ways in which seemingly beneficent systems such as schools, hospitals, and, yes, parks, are places of insidious violence against the oppressed.

82. Clifford, Pat and Tyrone Williams. *washpark*. delete press. 2021. 46.

Williams and Clifford's documentary poetical project is meant to be understood in this chapter as a juxtapositional production to that of Swensen's which has both informed my proscriptions and emblematizes the hypothesized though unexamined alternative output. Such outputs are assessed more thoroughly in the conclusive chapter of this book, where the matter of aesthetic production is also under examination.

83. ibid.

84. As is discussed elsewhere in this text, and is structurally inherent to its design and content, this particular ignorance is one of the grounds of the manifold crises today, which we treat as though can be *but part* of our cognitive occupations. This absence of more centralized and dominant focus on crises—especially as regards certain types of possible counterprogrammatical actions (political or aesthetical)—has both prevented much social change generally while also leading to an absence of general social upheaval with the second Trump administration. This is to speak of actions such as rioting, striking, and other widespread social disruption in order to demand immediate and direct action.

85. This is a misprision predicated on yet another institutional division regarding what is or is not understood as art, or, more

appropriately, in what venue the work of art is understood to be presencing itself or is disregarded as a possibility of there viable production.

86. *Ours*. 3.

87. Swensen, Cole. *Park*. Floating Island, 1991. 18.

88. ibid. 26.

89. Such belief is differentiated from compulsion to speak, as impulsed by the source of our Beingness.

90. **DIVAGATION**

Walking the dog / along the Parkway / drain covers—originating the world over / examine them: *Made in India*—so we've outsourced our industrial scale plumbing couverture to another country / it is 60 percent cheaper to manufacture manhole covers in Dasnagar, India and then import them to the United States / There are nearly 320 foundries in the Howrah Foundry Development Cluster / and nearly 15,000 people employed in the foundries / in the past decade, India has contributed substantial developments and innovations to urban sewer infrastructure (and its development) / Whereas earlier methods of filtration of sewer waste involved use of planted / New Sequencing Batch Reactors (SBRs) are but one machine implemented with a smaller footprint and faster replication time frame—not to mention its partial automation is fundamentally more capable of efficient implementation versus the heavy alterations to landscape and arena when constructing out-of-date sewage treatment facilities / While often overlooked, faecal sludge removal is of critical importance to hygienic maintenance for society / Additional factors to consider include: pollution et al / The Howrah Municipal Corporation proposed ~600,000USD of infrastructural improvements to drains, drain covers, and sewer diversions, to be implemented between 2013-2014 in available reports defining the plan and design for the use of corporate bidding to receive the project contracts / Many of the manhole covers called for in this development are likely locally produced by foundries mentioned above / In July of 2017, Pooja and Mukesh Verma lodged the following complaint with municipal authorities [as registered in a list-feed of transcribed complaints (in English)] *Sewer has been badly chocked blocked/overflow since 10 days and conditions are pathetic. The round lid is open and the sewege water is over flowing. and the sewer dirty water has been mixed in water supply and makes life difficult due to bad smell in water.* / Numerous similar complaints are registered also—by various other parties / Pooja and Mukesh Verma are in a protracted divorce commenced before late 2021 and continuing in court transfer [as registered on the docket of the Indian Supreme Court] in 2023 without resolution / Pooja Verma is a Punjabi actress / Pooja Verma is an MBA student in Michigan / *Pooja Verma is a young fashion designer based out of India* / Pooja Verma is an environmental and energy sector auditor / Mukesh Verma has a page on the US NIH website advertising and defining his role as Branch a Chief of the Epidemiology and Genomics Research Program / Another Mukesh Verma is a legislator in Uttar Pradesh / There is a LinkedIn page describing Mukesh Verma as a "Bollywood Director" active "since 1985" / The original complaint as registered is thus anonymous— / The following is a list of manhole cover types as advertised in a c2013 catalog produced for Kent Stainless, an Irish manufacturer primarily producing stainless steel products / These manhole covers are deployed across Ireland for various industrial usages, and mark significant examples not only of efficient capabilities—such as the single operator lifting models for heavy usage pumps and meters, for instance, which need covering—but of innovative capacity as well, with the specific bespoke capabilities of Kent Stainless contributing to their proclivity for innovation overall in the field / Necessity and mothers—you know the cliches are hunted as they emerge—perhaps excising portions of them will help protect them from the merciless Hunter, wherever they are? / :

External: / *Kent Solo Paver / Kent Multi Paver / Kent Hinges Solo Paver / Kent Hinged Multi Paver / Kent Paver Man Access / Kent Solo Telecover / Kent Multi Telecover / Kent Solo Chequer / Kent Multi Chequer / Kent Hinged Solo Chequer / Kent Hinged Multi Chequer / Kent Chequer Man Access / Kent Paver In Ground Power Unit / Kent Paver Recessed Tree Pit / Kent Perforated Dished Street Channel Grating / Kent Hinged Dished Ladder Street Grating / Kent Paver Slot Street Grating /* **Internal:** / *Kent Solo Internal Manhole / Kenti Multi Internal Manhole / Kent Hinged Internal Manhole / Kent Vinyl Manhole / Kent Hinged Vinyl Manhole*

This list only describes model classes and not specific model numbers, of which there are numerous for specific operations and fields / Alongside manholes, Kent's catalog describes grilles, external and internal / This concludes my comments on manholes and grilles / Though interesting developments would be available to those interested in continuing, such as the grids overlaid on images in the catalog without explication, or the various types of heel mesh—at which point individuals may also care to examine the numerous anti-terrorism offerings Kent Stainless *also* produces.

91. There is also a more recent book of poetical biographies or sketches of various notable art figures, some of whom are people of color or globalized minorities in relation to the order delineated by United States policy. However, even this text does not say very much regarding social conditions. *Art in Time* is the name of this collection. One sequence which glimpses the issues we describe in this chapter reads [Agnes] *Varda often focused on people often unheard— vagabonds, gleaners, cleaners, shopkeepers, villagers, with landscape framing, even enabling, character—Her late film* Visages, Villages *with the face of the French countryside moving smoothly behind, the one thing that binds all these otherwise disparate places and faces—"* (Swensen, Cole. Art in Time. Nightboat. 2021. 20.) This passage is quite telling towards the overall concern and perception, in Swensen, with and for the park and geography in France. For Swensen, here, we see that the view is that, perhaps, these features do somehow 'enable' the voice to appear of the 'unheard.' If we contemplate the nature of that unheard class, however, we see little save a very simplified guild-system of labor; we see occupations which render there an 'under-class.' These moments in Swensen texts appear just as this and subside, fleeting as they are—they do not linger nor become object of examination or change of authorial awareness.

92. *Ours*. 47.

93. This continues in *The Proposition* which came out in the Fall of 2024, marking one of the final works for which Hejinian has provided her own commentary.

In regards *My Life*—whose? (We are told). Most of us agree this is a great work of poetry, while fewer of us appear to deal with the documentation of Great American Whiteness—that mythos in tandem with the American Dream. Everything absent is the lived reality of suffering. For each truth has its un-truth…

94. *Ours*. 31.

95. A Program for Art?

> *There are different ways to approach any subject,*
> *and I did not want it to be a photojournalistic approach,*
> *and I did not focus on the famous people in the cemetery.*
> Bethany Jacobson on *Ode to a Cemetery*

Practically, we call for an ethics of looking and speaking in a society that is plagued by such persistent and violent inflictions upon the minoritized body, especially the non-white body. When a white body speaks in a manner that *refuses* to recognize the holistic of the quotidian—its violence—they are speaking non-sensically and preserving a false, supremacist image of reality: *their* history.

Swensen expressed in the question period for the Flow Chart Foundation's *Ode to a Cemetery* reading that she tends to focus in some ways on *ekphrasis*, on *writing on art*, but there too, considering the absencing of some certain people or bodies from the history of Western art (where her interest obviously lies), occurs an intense problematic for we have seen consistently the erasure of the truth of oppression throughout the history of art. Bodies are simply *not shown* there, and Swensen's work categorically does not attempt to resurrect what is absented. It only looks at what is there, the myth, the propaganda, and engages in it. Her work sustains the glorification of a white culturality across time, even where she may claim this is not the case in describing a different angle on historicization. Swensen was accused of racial bias by Anne Seaton, demonstrating that bias as essence-of-praxis in her response back to Seaton and that discussion. Her response [which is discussed in other notes] read in part that *overall my goal was not to address the social conditions of that age,* which I would argue extends to much of the social condition of any age under examination in what are multiple book-length historical lyric studies by Swensen—towards themes, subjects, and biographies.

One of my intentions with this chapter is to follow up the overall conversation to note not only agreement with the line of criticism and its wider urgency, but also to point out that Swensen's projects have an overall routine habit of fixating upon sanitized renditions of socially reactive subjects. Swensen had herself continued her rebuttal with the statement *perhaps there is no legitimate subject for poetry, indeed any art, other than social conditions, and perhaps we are at a moment in which this is particularly true.* ["Cole Swensen Responds" in *Jacket2*]. I would argue that this is the more astute observation, and I wish to take it at face-value as an earnest thought, although it bears sensations of irony or sardonicism as well.

As to that hesitation, take for instance, when writing of Renee Gladman in *Art in Time*, how Swensen makes the comment that *rising within is always a city whose name is always on the tip // recalibrating the angle of the hand poised over paper. (107).* This statement bifurcates between application towards the producer of the artwork under examination—Gladman's asemic texts—and the viewer—Swensen—where we can, on the viewer's side, recognize the role the extrinsic others around us play in re-visioning our/her perceptions—the recalibration; the chapter or poem is remarkably evocative of the Williams and Clifford collaboration (with the frequent mention of walking the city), but, towards the conclusion, we find the speaker (again, also in application to the producer, here Gladman—at which point we also note that the angle of analysis of the producer of the work of art functions totally differently than the application upon the viewer) going in a different direction, not recalibrating but consuming and re-presenting (as authority[?]): *We lived in the city as a matter of measuring. We lived in the city as a method of filtering. We filtered the finest grains of the slightest emanations we gathered from everything living, and distilled them* (111).

What is the ethical and political value of an aesthetical work describing the need for solace of a singular body, against the traumas and needs within hierarchical and realistic power structures [at times possibly being literally trodden over]? With community efforts showing substantial energy towards documenting and promoting the segregation of Green-Wood

Cemetery, especially efforts beginning more earnestly in the mid to late 2010s, against the 20th Century restoration efforts preserving the generally 'white' narrative history, we are able to witness a historical trajectory overall where subjects who are deprived of power and agency, and equity, are continuously left behind. Must we continue to justify and perpetuate production of art that seeks to capture a majestic purity of nature, stretching its hand and eye towards divinity (a divinity which implies an ordering to the nature of hatred and oppression, as well), or can we move into a revolutionary dynamic where the work of art extrapolates and deploys the urgent social changes we must be implementing in a totalized manner [across the board] in order to ensure the equity of all people? The United States of America, and the political and economic system it maintains, is averse to a programmatic overhaul of artistic production in terms of what is preserved, published, promoted, and maintained. At the same time, the abhorrent status quo, as well as the refusals to repair or recuperate against past genocidal wrongs, continues. This has led to the continued and contemporary necessity for creating new spaces to represent and promote underrepresented voices. It would seem that so long as people are being obliterated in their history and their attempts to communicate their needs and experiences, the noise created by a stultifying *white-supremacist* matter alongside the praise and consideration (discussion) the white work receives, would continue to create the necessity for making other spaces strictly exclusive to the underrepresented. The system as it stands, dominated by white institutions, continues to force inequity and non-plurality. We cannot find a diverse commons with this institutional paradigm.

96. Considering the return or recurrence of Trump back into the Presidential administration of the United States, regardless of Jared Kushner's participation or role, we should view there to be some continuity of Kushner's operations—predominantly in officiating or wooing purchasers of arms and other major military technologies. The United States is one of the two largest arms dealers in the world and is therefore responsible for an overwhelming amount of death and devastation [though, as seen even here, these government officials view such genocide as mere *destruction*—for it is themselves who can recuperate these lands, if only for their own cruel purposes.

An interesting text which has late contributed in furthering these thoughts can be found in *A Mutual Extortion Racket: The Military Industrial Complex and U.S. Foreign Policy—The Cases of Saudi Arabia and UAE*, which is freely available from *Transparency International Defense & Security Program*.

We also should recall that Kushner's official actions in the first Trump Administration continued, currying favor and relations with Saudi Arabia *after* the execution of Jamaal Kashoggi. Outside of an official government role, though platformed and benefitting from his government position and closeness to government power, Kushner continues such immoral/amoral/villainous alliances by making the above real estate property claims about Gazan waterfronts in the midst of the total obliteration of Palestine by the Zionist settler state.

97. During his legal proceedings and trials, Donald J Trump routinely received rights to both speedy trials and delayed trials so that he could feel things out and live his life—he had big

things planned, so why should a court be able to stop him? When Trump's sentencing was delayed so as 'not to influence the election,' there was minimal outrage from the liberal establishment. The Democrats have made a practice of alignment with institutional decorum and procedure, which they venerate beyond the needs of the polis—the social fabric they claim to be preservers of is State order guised as beneficial legislation. Meanwhile the GOP have exploited any system they can in order to deliver results for themselves and their voting base (and people wonder why the GOP remains popular). The reductive Democratic establishment routinely capitulates to Trump, as they have during the transition into his second term where they are making allowances about judicial appointments that the current administration holds claim over, ceding them to Trump. Even here, the Democrats ignore their judicial frustrations from the Right and outright ignore the fundamental judicial overhaul Trump's first administration enacted. The Democratic establishment has continued to establish and shore up Trump's plans and actions.

98. Toufic, Jalal. *Distracted*. 2nd Edition. Tuumba Press, 2003. 10-11.

99. ibid. 15.

100. ibid. 16. with *everything is an event, irrespective of eternal recurrence and the production of **the will***

101. ibid. 33.

102. both lines ibid. 122.

103. ibid. 31.

104. ibid. 9.

105. Osman, Jena. *The Network*. Fence Books, 2011. 27. See also: Osman, Jena. *A Very Large Array*. DABA. 2023. 26.

106. ironical further extension of the dynamic body as "hero" in posture to save/refuse life to, say, a drowning victim—that he is *entrusted* by the attendee/victim with their safety, and readily exploits it. At the same time, the lifeguard is *employed* or *in service* to the patrons, and transgresses the capitalist social contract of that space when declaring *I want to enjoy*—a revolutionary space, then, of liberating the worker from the workplace, enabling a democracy of experience in the space of the workday, no longer limited [of experience] to when one is "free" to act upon their desires or impulse

107. Within visual narratives, the location of *an answer* through such a totality as recording or surveillance equipment often appears as a moment of revelation or finality [the answer finally shown on screen and to the viewer], or else as cliffhanger—a moment to cut to advertisement, to b-story, and so forth to withhold the answer and build anticipation; there are other times where, either through this route or otherwise, the evidentiary equipment/technology of surveillance, has failed or is manipulated so it withholds the answer—still, there is no elision of the surveillance technologies evidentiary power, that it is site of proof and reality.

108. Toufic. *Distracted*. 43.

109. This book commences with the following disclaimer: A copy of this textbook is issued to each appointed elder, and he may retain it as long as he continues to serve as an elder in any congregation. At such time as he should cease to serve in that capacity, his copy of the book must be handed over to the Congregation Service Committee, since this publication is congregation property. No copies

are to be made of any part of this publication.

110. from Unit 2b, pg 39.

111. from Unit 1b, pg 23.

112. from Unit 5c, pg. 134.

113. This section was composed while watching videos and looking at news articles sharing the drone footage discussed and shown. In particular, the commentary shared here was of interest and the italics are drawn from this.

114. Transcript found at: https://www.govinfo.gov/content/pkg/CHRG-117shrg45209/html/CHRG-117shrg45209.htm

115. Perelman, Bob. *Braille*. Ithaca House, 1975. 44.

116. The value of the dramatic [which we determine as a factorial of different registers contextually], over some cases of the prosaic [κοινότοπος] is in part where the actor 'brings the character to life,' and in the process realizes them differently case to case. The character thus must have, in poietically derived drama, some plasticity to their backstory (sans radical departure that becomes reimagining), or else the imagination will be denied. The

staging or production of drama—its performance—in this enacted way is inherently poietical. At the same time, the reading of drama [as literature or aesthetic object, for instance] may or may not produce the effects of poietic language. Drama is comfortably not the terrain of totalizing detail, whereas the commonplace prosaic is that terrain or else it frustrates its operator (the technology [of writing/literature's user being the reader/audience]). Here, we outright regard the produced or staged drama as affording a glimpse at the venue of ἀλήθεια, as it relates to the function of poiesis and the affectation of the understanding of Being. The social awareness/witness [effecting re-mediation] in tandem arises through the aesthetical-functionary power this mode of art manifests. This is a situation that happens across en-acted dramatic production regardless the purported 'quality' or dynamic of its staging.

117. This chapter is meant as only an initial sketch or concept on the way towards the social revolution hypothesized both here and elsewhere. It is resultantly neither perfect nor final. Two expansions come to mind with some urgency—at least to suggest them. The first is a more prolonged discussion of the examples of poietic outputs across the array of genre and media. The second is the positing of either a synthetical fourth, pedagogical, register, or an expansion of the description of the quotidian domain of the technical and prosaic registers to describe the role pedagogy plays as both extension and destruction of the problematic components of non-poietic speech. There is substantial room for a merging of the poietic, technical, and prosaic when conducted under certain pedagogical conditions—with this being a space

for considering the realization of a new societally held speech..
Arguably, the suggestions or programs this chapter pushes towards are realizable largely, perhaps solely, through pedagogical praxis. This would be especially so for a pedagogy predicated on mediation in comparison to base interpretation. These and other developments of the present conception are the subject of (my) work that is ongoing in the aftermath of the present volume.

118. Many critiques of MFA poetry in the United States strive towards this delineation, where is a crystalline example of the poem's capacity to be instructed (versus the poiem, which can only be felt) and poetry's technological definitioning—entailing such an array of techniques and devices as: contest submissions, reading fees, use of Submittable, networking, professional editing of literary magazines, and so forth as part of a preconceived system of minimal "creation" and maximal reproduction. But these criticisms are unfair and target only a network of production viewed as privileged by outsiders. The case is such that "MFA poets," whatever that category may be—it does not adequately exist—are being instructed further within this technological domain, and may thus find their distance from the poietical widens.

119. Stein, Gertrude. *Lectures in America*. Beacon Press, 1985. 231.

120. Hence the re-mediatory role, given purely stated speaking, the poietical, is *after* another speaking that is heard, while exegesis is not explicitly re-mediatory but definition, seeking to capture what was heard and re-express it's essence.

121. All quotes from Levertov are via

Levertov, Denise. *The Jacob's Ladder*. New Directions, 1961.

122. This has substantial relation to entertainment and amusement as distraction, which should be explored in elaborating but one aspect of the danger of technology within the contemporary.

123. Therein also has happened the deployment of the prior works' content into impact on the recipient.

CLOAK

Learn more at https://cloak.wtf

ISBN: 979-8-218-64331-7

www.ingramcontent.com/pod-product-compliance
Lightning Source LLC
Chambersburg PA
CBHW061147160726
48006CB00038B/2305